THE NEW ORATORY

ANTONY JAY

THE NEW
ORATORY

Illustrated by Alnos Hall

American Management Association, Inc.

International standard book number: 0-8144-5259-0

Library of Congress catalog card number: 71-152037

Second Printing

Published in Great Britain under the title
*Effective Presentation: The Communica-
tion of Ideas by Words and Visual Aids*

Preface

It was only in about 1964 that I discovered presentations. Until then I had been a full-time television producer and writer for the BBC, believing that I was one of a very small group of people who were grappling with the problem of employing a wide range of audio-visual techniques to present facts, ideas, and arguments. But in 1964 I became a free lance, and quite soon I was invited to produce a presentation for an industrial company. From then on the pace quickened, and I began to realize that all over the Western world (and for all I know the Eastern world as well) thousands, maybe tens of thousands, of presentations were being given and attended every day. Research groups presenting new projects to development committees, companies presenting them to government, salesmen presenting products to customers, advertising agencies presenting campaign ideas to clients, boards presenting new organizations or policies to executives, and all of them presenting things to the press and the public.

Almost as soon as the extent of this new industry

dawned on me, I realized that it was rooted in exactly the same craft that I had been practicing for the past ten years. Of course there were no television cameras or telecine machines or microphone booms, but these are only the trappings and the suits of television anyway. At the heart of my kind of factual, documentary television was the essential problem of the presentation: how to put over to small groups of people (the television audience is small groups, too, even if there are several million of them) new facts and ideas, in an attractive, interesting, and persuasive way, by the simultaneous use of words and pictures.

Obviously I started with something of an advantage: This problem had been my full-time professional preoccupation for ten years, and I had discussed almost every aspect of it endlessly with my colleagues on production teams. Moreover, for six of those years I had worked on a 40-minute, five-nights-a-week news/documentary/current affairs program calling, at one time or another, on every audio-visual technique and narrative device. Even so it came as a surprise, when going outside the walls of the television studio, to find how little thought or discussion had been given to the problems and principles of presentations by those who had to devise and make them. Industry, which seemed to be flooded with expert advisers on cost accounting, work study, operational research, media selection, press relations, resource management, production control, personnel motivation, and almost every other specialist and even nonspecialist activity, had desperately few helpers of even the most modest competence in the field of presentations—and no corpus of professional knowledge at all. For this reason it is hardly surprising that it is difficult to go to any presentation without encountering the most elementary errors of conception and execution. Much more surprising is the patient tolerance of the audiences who sit through them in charitable silence with a politeness that approaches the heroic.

It is now six years since I started producing and advising on presentations, and for most of that time I have found that there are certain basic points which I have had to make again and again—points which we hammered out in the 1950s in session after session of program autopsies until we had forged, at least to our own satisfaction, a basic grammar of audio-visual communication. Many times I have wished that there was a book embodying this grammar to which I could refer those who were about to embark on a presentation. I have finally become resigned to the necessity of writing it myself, if only to save the trouble of saying it all over again for another six years.

If anyone has picked up this book in the hope of a crackling philosophical discourse on the nature of human communication in modern industrial society, I advise him to put it down at once. It is no more than a brief and very humble operating manual for those who at some time or another have to present ideas, decisions, facts, or proposals to others in a context which demands something slightly more prepared and worked out than a chat over a drink, and who believe that it is worth spending some time and trouble to achieve maximum clarity, conciseness, impact, and persuasion—or at least to avoid alienation, catastrophe, and humiliation.

—A.J.

Contents

1 / Introduction

What is a presentation? To start with, it is not a lesson, and a presenter cannot think of his role in terms of a teacher's. None of his audience are going to sit at an examination and answer questions on what he has been telling them. He cannot set them homework, or give individual attention to the backward pupils, or stop and give a quick test to see who has been paying attention. Moreover, one of the most important of the teacher's techniques is almost always denied to him—the technique of involving the class, making them do things for themselves, keeping them busy. There is of course a strong element of presentation in class instruction, for which I hope these chapters will be useful, but handling the class is more important and deserves a book which I am certainly not competent to write.

Less obvious, and for that reason perhaps more important, is the fact that a presentation is not a lecture. They look alike, there is rarely any class activity in a lecture, and lectures employ all the visual techniques discussed in this book. Nevertheless, there is a crucial difference— and it lies in the reason why the audience is there. A lecturer can reasonably assume (even if the best of them do not) that his audience arrives with a desire, or at least a need, to know what he is going to tell them. A presenter's audience is in almost every case invited by him or his organization; his need to impart information is usually greater than his audience's need to receive it. Moreover, the lecturer is usually to some extent the servant of a syllabus. If something is particularly complicated, he just has to take the extra time to try and elucidate it: He does not have the same freedom as the presenter to choose what to put in and what to leave out.

If one must find a parallel from another profession, a presenter is much closer to an advocate than to a teacher or lecturer. A presentation is an exercise in persuasion. Of course there are other ingredients—the communication of information and ideas—but the presentation takes place in order to persuade a person or group of people to adopt or revise an attitude, to accept or modify an opinion, to take or refrain from taking an action or decision. Of course teachers and lecturers have the same need to persuade, but in a presentation it is more overt.

In most presentations, too, the normal speaker-audience relationship is reversed. If one man stands up on his own to address a crowd of other men, there is an implication that his status is in some way superior to theirs (this is dealt with more fully in Chapter 7), but in a presentation it is usually the other way round: The speaker addresses his audience respectfully as a subordinate among men of higher status. He cannot demand their attention—the most he can do is to deserve it. A normal consequence of this is that the duration of the presentation is restricted. A lecturer may ask himself, "How long does the subject need?" but the presenter's first question is usually, "How long can the audience spare?"

A presentation is an exercise in persuasion.

The logic of limited time leads to certain inescapable conclusions. Obviously the presenter, like the lecturer, wants to use the time to maximum advantage, and this involves taking trouble. The lecturer can share the trouble with his class, he can give them extra reading or writing or practical work, or he can force them to concentrate hard while he is lecturing. The presenter takes all the trouble himself to save his audience trouble; he makes things hard for himself so that they may be easy for his audience.

One consequence of this is the need for visual aids. You cannot compress words beyond a certain limit without losing the comprehension and interest of your audience, but a judicious use of pictures can communicate the same information not only enormously faster but also much more effectively and memorably. And, once visual aids are included, the exposition starts to become more formal in the strict sense of having to keep to a prearranged form. A talk can wander about in a general way on the basis of a few points in the speaker's head or a few notes on his crib card, but he departs from the order of a slide sequence at his peril.

It may seem that the presentation is a form of communication which is walled about with restrictions and loaded with burdens. It does, however, have one liberating factor: It is usually only required to be a prelude to further discussion and exposition. If it fails, that further discussion will not take place; but, if it succeeds, the audience to whom it was given will want to study the subject in more detail. Its objective is limited; it does not have to be comprehensive. Usually a presentation is successful if it arouses curiosity and stimulates a desire for more information; the desire can be satisfied in other ways and at other times.

2 / Planning the Presentation: Thinking It Out

It is a general law applicable to any project that the earlier a mistake is made the more profoundly it affects the whole project and the harder it is to recover from. Presentations are no exception. If there is a misconception, or an omission, or an error of intent built into the beginning of a presentation, then all the subsequent time and thought and work are doomed. For this reason there should be a fair amount of exploratory discussion, with at least three people in the case of a presentation in which a number of individuals will participate, at the very beginning. Chapter 4, on the schedule, deals with the question of what meetings are necessary and who should attend; at the moment we are concerned with what must be done.

Although this section deals with the presentation as a whole, the separate stages have to be followed by each individual presenter when he approaches his subsection of the whole presentation—as well as by the planner of a one-man presentation at the start of his task.

The earlier a mistake is made the more profoundly it affects the whole project and the harder it is to recover from.

Start from First Principles

Formulate a precise objective. The first question to ask is why you are giving the presentation at all. It is easy to come up with a general "waffle" answer; the aim is to narrow it down to a single sentence defining a precise and limited objective. You can say, "To improve the corporation's return on employed assets," but that is everyone's business all the time. You can say, "To sell more computer time," which is getting warmer, but what is the whole sales force for? All right—"To remove some of the doubts and misgivings about computer time sharing from the minds of potential customers in professional partnerships and small companies." *Which* doubts and misgivings? That the equipment will break down? That it won't work? That it is too expensive? That people won't use it? The more of this sort of questioning you subject yourself to at this stage, the more you sharpen the point of the whole presentation. It is worth writing out your final objective in a single sentence: "To show the members of medium-size professional firms in accountancy and engineering consultancy that a time-sharing computer terminal is something they need and can afford, that programming is much easier than they think, and that the equipment is reliable and easy to operate." You should make sure, too, that everyone sees this objective—and sees it the moment he is recruited to the presentation team. It should become the touchstone against which you test anything that may or may not deserve inclusion.

Identify the audience. The second part of thinking it out, although separate, is intimately bound up with the first, and you cannot begin to formulate any part of the presentation until this too has been thrashed out. I have to put them on paper consecutively, but in your mind they have to proceed in parallel. If you ask, "What are we trying to convey?" you must also ask, "To whom are we trying to convey it?" For this you have to try and get inside the minds of your audience. What are they thinking about the subject? To be quite basic, how much do they already know about computers? What is the level of their technical interest and understanding? Have they ever used computers? What unfortunate experiences have they had with them or heard or read about? How up to date are they on the latest models? Is it the concept of time sharing they are resisting, or are they simply deciding between us and our competitors?

All this has to be thrashed out just as thoroughly as the objective. If you are in serious doubt, it is worth having a session with someone who will be one of the audience, or who at least comes from the same group (for example, accountant, engineer, architect, research scientist), and trying to discover from him the level of interest, information, understanding, experience, prejudice, and resistance that you should expect to find in your audience. Finally you should be able to formulate another key sentence—the one which expresses the final impression you want to leave in the minds of your audience when the presentation ends. Again you must limit it: Should it be, "I must remember to order one of the things tomorrow morning"? Or just, "Perhaps these things can help us after all—I must set up a committee to look into the matter properly"?

These two thought processes may sound obvious, and indeed everybody who plans a presentation goes through them in some sort of way. The reason for emphasizing them here is that in most cases the process is carried out in a hasty and desultory manner, and abandoned while the objective is still inadequately formulated and the audience too vaguely identified. For a successful presentation, at least two hours need setting aside for questions, suggestions, arguments, and the formulation of exact objectives—two exhausting hours of hard thinking. When you consider how much more time is going to be spent on scripts and rehearsals and aids in the days to come, this is a small amount to allot to constructing the foundations that everything else will be built on.

Plan the Ingredients

Quite simply, what shall we include? This is the obvious bit that everyone can do. A few tips:

• Simply for the production discipline, write down the point each section is making. Not simply "range" but "range of programs now available and further programs in preparation."

• Even at this early stage, put duration against each section and subsection—it helps to give early warning of overcrowding.

• For further help, sort out the various possible ingredients into A, B, and C columns: A for what must be included, B for what ought to be, and C for what it would be worth saying if there were time.

• Having noted all the points you want to include, form them into a logical sequence in which the points you are trying to make succeed each other most naturally. If you like, you can suggest speakers (provided there is more than one speaker) and durations. The following is a sample of logical sequence that will show what I mean.

A. Chairman (Introduction)

1. Computing now universal. In big firms the clerical savings on payroll, invoicing, and sales analysis justify the outlay on their own. But small professional partnerships—accountants, engineers, architects—who need computing just as much cannot cover the outlay by staff savings.
2. A bureau is not the answer—you can't wait 24 hours and then discover you made a program error. Want answer now. Minicomputer not the answer—some of the computing very complex and high-powered; wide range of programs needed.
3. Remote direct-access terminal is best of both worlds. Teletypewriter in the office linked by telephone line to big central computer many miles away.

Total   10 min.
Running Total   10 min.

B. Sales Director

4. Will demonstrate in a moment. First, the economics. Rent of equipment. Line costs. Pay for computer time only when using it. Costs. Program storage. Sharing with sixty other subscribers. Reduced off-peak rates.
5. Conversational relationship with computer. Computer asks the questions.

D.C.F. (*discounted cash flow*) *Demonstration*

6. Outline standard programs available without extra charge.

Total   20 min.
Running Total   30 min.

C. Chief Programmer

7. Brief explanation of principle of time sharing and program storage and retrieval. Security.

8. Writing your own programs.

   Demonstration: Investment allowance program

Total	15 min.
Running Total	45 min.

D. CUSTOMER (ACCOUNTANT)

9. Practical applications. "Teething" troubles. Lessons learned. Pitfalls. Summary of advantages to date. Planned developments for future.

Total	10 min.
Running Total	55 min.

E. CHAIRMAN (SUMMARY)

10. Growth of time sharing. Compare with telephones. Big firms need own exchange, smaller ones just want own phone and a line to central exchange.
11. Comparative cost/benefit analysis with computer ownership. Flexibility—you can get out if you don't like it. Recruitment advantages. Reliability record. U.S. statistics. End story.

Total	10 min.
Final Running Total	1 hr. 5 min.

Once the logical sequence is worked out, everyone should have a copy of it. It is important that all those who are going to give parts of the presentation be well acquainted with everybody else's theme as well before they start to think about what they want to say. This is a great help in preventing gaps or overlap.

Decide on Structure

If the first two stages have been properly completed, we know what we want to say, why, in what order, and to whom. Now we have to decide how to structure it.

Surely we have done that already with our logical sequence? No, we have not. The chief purpose of the logical sequence was to clear up in our own minds the progression of the argument. We will probably follow the thread of it more or less, but we now have to add something else: the storyteller's art. So far all we have produced is a logical argument; we have to turn it into an interesting talk or series of talks.

The word "talk" is significant, and talk is the subject of Chapter 5. This is a spoken presentation and not a written paper. For this reason, any presenters who are inexperienced in writing for speech should, when they have structured their talks, speak them into a tape recorder and have them transcribed rather than write them out.

Give some thought to duration. Most people are worried that they will not have enough to say. There seems to be some sort of guilt about giving short measure. Consequently, the great danger at this stage is of having too much. It is not a bad idea to use the A, B, and C principle and to mark each paragraph of your draft script (and other speakers' if any) with the appropriate grade. You can then cut the "C" paragraphs without too much trouble. Cutting at the draft-outline stage is easy, but it becomes more and more painful as time goes on and further thought and time and care are put into the presentation. Always aim to run significantly short at this stage. More ideas will come later; the presentation will "spread" when you actually use the visual aids, and so what if a morning's presentation is twenty minutes short? You've presumably said what you want, and the extra length of coffee and pre-lunch breaks won't upset anybody. By contrast, a presentation that runs too long upsets everyone. People try to go too fast, anticipated breaks are delayed and curtailed and it is always the more interesting but less essential parts that get cut and consequently make the whole presentation more indigestible.

Work at your opening. The first few minutes of the presentation are extremely important in a way that has nothing to do with its content. There is a folklore belief that you should always start with a joke. Like so many folklore beliefs, it is not true, but there is truth somewhere at the root of it. The fact is that every speaker needs some sort of acceptance from the audience: If they are to accept what you say, they need some grounds for believing that you are in most ways the same sort of person they are. A good joke that is not obtrusively dragged in, that is relevant and amusing and gets a big laugh, is an excellent way of giving them this sense of all belonging to the same tribe (see Chapter 6). However, a joke that fails has exactly the reverse effect and may be very hard to recover from. An opening joke is therefore particularly dangerous if your audience is very small, if it is unfamiliar, or if ever you have doubts about whether it will get the laugh you intend. There are many alternatives: any expression of genuine personal feeling, some honest self-revelation (especially of the self-deprecating kind which shows you are an ordinary chap like the rest of them and not setting yourself up as a superior person)—any of these approaches to the audience can help to create an "accepting" kind of atmosphere. This of course is true not just for the start of the whole presentation but also for any new presenter's opening remarks.

"Connect up" with the audience. There is another reason for particular care with the first few minutes, and it is related to what I have already said. It is here that you harness the horse of your argument to the wagon of the audience's interest and understanding. If you gallop straight off, you may hurtle along splendidly without

realizing you left them all behind at the starting gate. You have to start in the area they know and understand, you have to identify correctly the assumptions and questions in their minds before you can start to take them with you into unknown territory. This cannot be done in a couple of sentences, but it is complementary to demonstrating that you are the same sort of person they are because, in talking about *their* experience and problems rather than *your* knowledge and ideas, you are getting their confidence that you understand them, that you are in touch and worthy to be granted a further hearing. After all, they expect you to have the right answers. What you have to demonstrate is that you have the right questions.

Make them want to know. A computer salesman once explained to me, rather convincingly, why his job was very like a missionary's or an evangelist minister's. Both he and they, he said, succeeded by discovering or implanting some unease or guilt or fear in the person they were trying to convert. He himself did not deal in hell fire and torment. He was concerned only with business rivals doing things more cheaply or better or more quickly and some people being left behind by the technological revolution, but he felt that the principle was the same: Nobody was interested in salvation until he had a fear of damnation. I am not suggesting anything so extreme; nevertheless, if the audience is rather cool it is a great help if you can make them aware, from the very start, of the ways in which what you are about to present is important to them. They arrive prepared to listen; by the end of the first ten minutes they should be wanting to know.

Keep relating to the audience. The principle of connecting up with the audience also applies at the end of each section of every presentation. When a point is made and you reach a pause, think of your listeners' minds again. What question or reflection will be occupying them now? At this stage, of course, you need only a sentence or so ("This is all very well, but it doesn't answer the question . . ."). However, it is a very important structural sentence because it also serves another useful purpose: that of "signposting," which is dealt with in Chapter 5, and it helps to prevent the presentation from becoming an unbroken string of factual assertions, which after a time becomes very hard to listen to.

The value of narrative. If you see yourself in danger of falling into the factual-assertion trap, remember the value of narrative. You may be describing a piece of equipment and find yourself saying, "This part does this . . . This part does this . . ." and so on, in a number of different ways, for far too long. You can often improve this sort of description enormously by turning it into a story: "Designing the projector was an intriguing problem. To start with, it had to be portable, so . . . but that meant we couldn't . . . so we tried. . . . Finally we hit on . . . and then we ran into another snag. . . . Meanwhile, the optical group had come up with an ingenious. . . ." And so a dull specification is turned into an interesting narrative.

Don't be too comprehensive. Remember that this is only a presentation. It does not have to be comprehensive. Build it only out of things that will interest the audience as a whole. Do not include anything tedious, or beyond most of them, or too detailed, because it "ought" to be included or because one or two may want to know. You can supply any amount of supporting documentation for them to study at their leisure, referring them to it at the appropriate point.

Further Practical Decisions

At this stage you should also decide whom to invite, what size the audience should be, and where to hold the presentation. You will find some helpful tips on these matters later on in this book, particularly in Chapters 7 and 8.

At this point you should not be worrying too much about visual aids. Of course, it may be that some demonstration is integral to the presentation and will be built in from the start; but excellent presentations can be given with no visual aids whatever, whereas no amount of help can turn a badly conceived and badly structured presentation into a good one. By now you should already have the makings of a good presentation; the purpose of visual aids is to make it even better. That is what the next chapter is about.

3 / Planning the Presentation: The Uses of Staging

All right, so we have decided what to say and worked out an interesting way of saying it. Need we do any more planning work?

The answer is no. If we have done most things right so far, we have a good basic exposition, and we can go ahead with it as it stands. But almost certainly we can do better: By starting to think about visuals, we can find ways of making what we say more intelligible, more interesting, more vivid, and more memorable. We may even find ways of making it entertaining and enjoyable. Moreover, at the back of our minds there is a feeling which Dr. Samuel Johnson once expressed: "This was a good dinner enough, to be sure; but it was not a dinner to *ask* a man to." We are afraid that although we have devised a good presentation enough, it is not a presentation to ask an audience to. In fact, so long as we put the right sort of thought into what we say and take the proper care over how we say it, those fears are often unfounded, and adding visuals just for visuals' sake will do more harm than good. Nevertheless, if we provide visible as well as audible evidence of the care and trouble we have taken, it is an additional act of courtesy to our audience; and it is more than likely that by adding another dimension to the presentation we can improve it significantly.

This is the impresario stage. So far we have thought of the audience as listeners to an address. Now we start to see them as spectators at a show. We look for points where interest sags, where the argument is complicated or lengthy, and think how we can lift our performance to a higher interest and enjoyment level. We start to look for ingredients which we have hitherto omitted on the basis of low relevance priority but which we should now reinstate on the basis of high interest priority. We study the presentation to find the points where the most interesting items should be placed.

This stage has to be approached with care; it is demanding of time and thought, and if mishandled it can turn what would have been a competent presentation into a disaster. But it can also upgrade a competent presentation into a first-class one. The difference is *purpose*. If all changes and additions now made are made for worked-out reasons based on the audience's mood, they are likely to work. If made because "we ought to make more of a presentation of it," they will destroy good work done so far. Better omit this stage than go through with it for the wrong reasons.

You still want to go on? Right. But don't say I didn't warn you.

On the whole, the longer the presentation the more important this stage becomes. Fifteen minutes, and you don't have to worry too much. Three hours, and this is a major part of the planning. Also, the larger the audience the more important this part. Yet even short presentations to small audiences can be greatly improved by a proper impresario approach.

This approach should be directed toward seven key areas.

1. Texture

By texture I mean only the different ways of addressing the audience. One man talking solidly, alone and unaided, for two hours presents an insufficiently varied texture. Texture is varied by film, sound tapes, demonstrations, visual aids, other speakers, questions, and, indeed, any other method of communication.

To study texture, forget about content and just look at what the audience is getting in terms of *means* of communication. Is there too much solid talk at any point? Will everyone be punch drunk with slide sequences? Are the demonstrations wasted by being too close together— could they be split up? Do things get too jumpy and bitty?

It's hard to write rules: What you need is an instinct for the boring. Once you've spotted a dull patch, it's not too hard to do something about it. Drop it, for instance— and reshape it as a supporting document.

At this stage, be prepared to make cuts and order changes—but don't lose hold of the main purpose. You are studying the means of communication, but what is being communicated is still what matters. The medium is not the message, except to the deaf. The medium is the envelope, and you are concerned with the letter inside. You should worry if Marshall McLuhan collects envelopes.

One man talking solidly, alone and unaided, for two hours presents an insufficiently varied texture.

A good practice is to go to a fairly big presentation that you're not particularly interested in and mark each stage "A," "B," or "C" for "interesting," "adequate," or "dull." It's easier to be ruthlessly honest about other people's presentations. But you will start to develop an instinct which you can apply to your own efforts.

It ought to be said at this stage that a really first-class speaker who knows his subject and his audience can in some circumstances hold his audience spellbound for an hour or more. But all too few of us have or can call upon such talent, and all too many of us have to manage without.

2. Attention Curve

Attention curves connect closely with texture. Psychologists have plotted how the attention of an audience or class varies during a forty-minute period. It starts high, drops fairly shallowly for the first ten minutes, then drops more steeply until it reaches its lowest point after about thirty minutes. Then it starts to rise steeply and is high again for the last five minutes. There are three points which follow from this:

• A shorter "period"—say twenty-five or thirty minutes —contains a higher percentage of high attention (though of course too many too short sections become self-defeating).

• Your most important points for the audience to remember must be at the beginning and end. In particular, the last picture and sentence or phrase of each period, which stay in the mind for a little longer before new words and images are piled on top, are especially important.

• Since attention diminishes after the first ten minutes, it is in that period, until it climbs again, that the greatest care must be devoted to texture variation and all other devices to revive and retain attention.

3. Breaks and Session Lengths

Again, breaks and session lengths are closely related to texture and the attention curve. A question session is not a break—it is a texture variation and is dealt with in the section on the audience. A break means the audience can get up out of their seats.

First of all, try and think how many times you have been sorry that a seminar or presentation has reached a break. Now think how many times you have been glad. If you're honest, the ratio is probably 1:10,000.

So breaks are a high point, and most presentations have too few, and sometimes they are too long. Much better have two of ten minutes than one of twenty. A morning presentation of three hours is much better divided by two short refreshment breaks, one after the first hour and another after the second, than by a single one (even if longer) after one and a half hours.

Finally, try and make each session end on a high note, if only to have the audience saying to each other "Quite good, isn't it?" over their coffee.

If sessions are not of equal length, then in principle the longest should be first and the shortest last, to combat the cumulative effect of successive sessions.

4. A Peep Behind the Curtain

A peep behind the curtain does not apply quite so much to the very large presentation with the full printed program; but in all other cases you have to remember that, although you know what is coming, the audience may not. So always cheer them up by telling them if there are some goodies in store. "In just a moment I'll be showing you some interesting pictures we took. . . ." "I've got one of the machines here, and later on I'll see if I can get this effect. . . ." "This has in fact been filmed, and during this session you'll be seeing. . . ." The mere presence of interesting-looking boxes on the table, or of easels with flip charts, perks up interest wonderfully. Remember, too, that attention peaks as you move over to start a demonstration, so between the "Right! Let's see if we can start the machine up" and the actual turning of the switch is an excellent moment to make a point you want everyone to take in.

5. Audience Participation

Apart from the fact that there are no disciplinary sanctions, it is the absence of "class activity," of the audience's participation, that makes the great difference between a lesson and a presentation. Participation, trying it out for yourself, is at the root of instruction. Because it is not there, the presenter is perhaps closer to the professional entertainer than to the teacher. But, having said that, I do not mean to imply that the presenter should not jump at any chance which arises to involve the audience.

A joke is the most obvious example. A joke is not funny until it is laughed at; it is completed by the laugh, and by laughing the audience is participating in the joke. The television-studio audience is a part of the show in a way that the viewer sitting at home smiling quietly to himself is not.

But a joke that is not laughed at is a major disaster, and not everyone has the confidence or the technique to go for laughs. What else? Well, sometimes you can get mental activity going on the lines of "How many wheels can you see in this picture?" but it doesn't happen much. There is, however, one opportunity which is too often neglected, and that is to give them something to hold—and if possible to keep. Any small cheap object which is reasonably relevant will do. In a computer presentation, a forty-column or eighty-column punched card and a small strip of magnetic or paper tape can be helpful and interesting and a most valuable variant. You don't have to deal them out to everyone—a pack to pass along each row is enough. It gets harder with more than a hundred people, but you can make up a small folder and put one on each seat in advance.

6. Impact

It can be helpful to think of visual aids as falling into three categories: (a) explanatory, (b) corroborative, and (c) memorable or "impact" visuals.

You will have included your explanatory visuals from the start. They are the ones you cannot really manage without—the sort of thing that is impossible to explain in words but easy with a picture or diagram or model.

When you were thinking about texture and the attention curve, you started looking for corroborative visuals. They were not a structural necessity; but they gave useful visual evidence, they backed up your argument, and they helped to lift the interest at a point where it was likely to be flagging.

Impact visuals are the ones most often forgotten. They answer the question, "What pictures do we want the audience to carry away in their minds?" Quite possibly they will be pictures already used for explanatory or corroborative reasons, but very probably they will not. In this case they need to be thought out with great care and placed in key positions—often the first or last thing in their session—and perhaps left up through the subsequent break. There is an Eastern proverb that goes like this: "I hear and forget, I see and remember, I do and understand." A presentation audience will not have much scope for doing and understanding, but they will do a great deal of hearing and forgetting. They will, however, remember what they see. You must make sure they see everything you want them to remember.

Under the heading of "impact" come all those devices for waking the audience up, surprising them, making them more alert and receptive. The best *coup de théatre* I know of is the army officer's lecture about surprise in warfare. He announced the subject, placed a tiny squib on the table, and got out his matchbox. As he was opening it, an accomplice detonated the most enormous thunderflash at the *back* of the audience. People leapt into the air as one man, and three points about surprise (deception about time, deception about place, deception about strength) were indelibly engraved on their memory.

7. Casting

Who should deliver the presentation? To start with, should it be one person or several? On the whole, I am for variety so long as there is some logic in it. If the audience cannot see why B should have taken over for A at this stage, then it would be better for A to have done it all himself; but, so long as it is clear that we

are now in an area where B has more skill or knowledge
or experience or authority, that's fine. A thornier question
in large organizations, particularly with what is basically
a one-man presentation, is this: What happens if the
senior man is not nearly as good at presentation as one
of his juniors? My own view is that the better presenter
must do the presentation, but that his superior should
start off the proceedings with a brief introduction and
end them with a short summary.

If the presentation is at all important, all the people
making significant contributions should have understudies. Certainly the chief presenter must have one. The
understudy's role is most important: He provides an extra
check on all the visual and stage-management details,
he can discuss improvements with the presenter, and he
can often avert disaster on the day by spotting that something is missing from the dais or that the slides are out
of order. The knowledge that he will have to do it all
himself if illness strikes sharpens his observation and
reactions wonderfully. (The shrewd presenter will com-
plain to his understudy of a slight headache and shivering
the evening before the presentation.)

If you are in charge of the whole presentation, and
especially if it is a large one, it is most unwise to take
part in it yourself. Apart from the fact that you have
quite enough to do already, there is another reason. Some-
body must constantly be devising, amending, assessing,
and judging the presentation exclusively from the point
of view of the audience. Anyone who is actually appearing in it will be at least partially preoccupied with his
own performance; moreover, his ego will make it impossible for him to be quite dispassionate about whether it's
his piece that is the letdown point in the whole presentation. Also, if you appear yourself it is harder to give help-

ful criticism and advice to the others—you and they will both sense that you are telling them they're not as good as you are. If this suspicion does not soften your criticism, then it will harden their resistance; either way it will impair your effectiveness.

The final and most important principle in all the planning stages is this: Never assume that the audience is going to be interested in the subject of your presentation. Expect them to be neutral—neither interested nor bored, but quite capable of being either. Unless you devote time and thought to the basic problem of keeping them interested, they can only too easily lapse into a boredom that is only a very short step from resentment.

4 / The Schedule

In a sense it is unnecessary to provide a schedule—it's fairly obvious what has to be done. Moreover a great many presentations are arranged with less time than they need, and some have to be mounted at a day or two's notice and are extremely successful. Nevertheless I have found over the years that there are certain key meetings which need to be held, and if any of them are not held then chances of success are noticeably reduced. A short and simple presentation with experienced presenters can combine some of these meetings, but the stages still have to be gone through. So it seemed best to list all the meetings which in an ideal world would take place before an important presentation. There are seven of them.

1. Purpose: What Shall We Do?

This meeting is for the decisions made when formulating the purpose and aims of the presentation (see Chapter 2). When they are clear, this meeting should decide who should actually take part in the presentation and what the role of each person should be. It is hard to say who should be at this meeting, but as a general rule you need at least three people—the basic presentation team: (1) the person in charge of the presentation; (2) an expert on the subject of the presentation, the product, plan, service, or whatever is being presented (probably a presenter too); (3) an expert on the object of the presentation, the needs and hopes and apprehensions and suspicions of the audience (probably a presenter too).

Action. Invite those who are required to take part in the presentation to the next meeting, with their understudies.

2. Content: What Shall We Say?

This meeting can be combined with the meeting just mentioned—but all the stages still have to be worked through. This requires the basic team and all other presenters and understudies. It is important at this stage to let everyone know how many more meetings there will be and what will be required of them at each stage, so that they don't try and jump straight to the end at once.

The members of the presentation team brief the presenters on background, aims, approach, and all practical details. They discuss with the presenters the general shape of the presentation, and the sort of thing each presenter should say and show. Each presenter should go off with a clear single sentence in his mind of what the audience should be thinking at the end of his address.

Action. All presenters write out notes of what they propose to include in their address and send them to the presentation team before the next meeting.

3. *Briefing the Presenters*

We are now moving from Chapter 2 to Chapter 3. This is a full presentation team meeting as in the preceding section. It is an excellent idea, if at all possible, to invite to this meeting someone who will be in the audience, or at least who comes from the group that will be attending the presentation, and reacts in the same way.

This meeting goes through the presenters' notes in order to

• Eliminate contradictions, overlapping points, and duplication.

• See if there are any gaps that no one has covered.

• Scrutinize all the proposed addresses from the point of view of the audience, so that the presenters can shorten sections that are familiar, amplify the more interesting and unfamiliar, simplify or drop the too technical or detailed, avoid irritations, and be aware where they are most likely to encounter resistance or disbelief. (This is the most important point.)

• Build in the other general points about structuring the addresses for audience interest as described in Chapter 3.

The presenters should leave this meeting with a clear and accurate sense of the audience they will encounter.

Action. Presenters dictate (or write out—see Chapter 5) what they want to say, with strict instructions that when delivered at a normal pace it will not go on for more than two-thirds of the speaking time allotted to them. Send these drafts in before the next meeting, with ideas for visuals.

4. Production Sessions

These are not full sessions. Ideally there should be a separate one for each presenter. With him should be the person running the presentation and at least one "production manager," responsible for all slides, film, microphones, charts, and indeed all technical equipment and details of practical organization. Depending on circumstances, you may also need a graphic designer, film or still photographer, projectionist, stage designer, lighting expert, and various other specialists. If the presentation is to be in a public building (such as a cinema, theater, or hotel conference room) a representative of their technical staff at these sessions can save a good deal of trouble later.

This is the meeting discussed in Chapter 3, where each address is studied for its impact and its dramatic, audience-holding qualities. Impact visuals are now discussed. All photographs, film, charts, drawings, models, equipment, and aids of every description are listed and their design worked out.

Action. The presenter must now finally turn his draft into a talk (see Chapter 5). But he must be sure not to turn his transcript into a paper; he must make his changes on the basis of his "spoken" document. The production manager sets in motion the design and execution of all visual aids and makes sure that everything is completed and ready for the next meeting. (It never is, but you have to try.)

Except in the simplest of presentations there will usually be a gap of at least two weeks, and quite possibly four, between this meeting and the next.

5. *The Stagger-through*

The stagger-through has acquired its name because run-through suggests a speed and smoothness which is a practical impossibility at this stage. This is the first bringing together of the presenter's final scripts with all their visual material and aids, and an attempt is made to go through them in sequence. As in production sessions, it should be done in separate sessions with each presenter. This is the time to discover and correct errors in the execution of visuals, to come up against technical difficulties of lighting and movement and operation, and to time the script and make cuts if necessary. A stopwatch comes in handy at this stage.

Here too it helps tremendously if someone who will be in the audience can come along and comment, from the consumer's point of view. This can also be done at the run-through, but the stagger-through gives more time for changes.

Action. Make any necessary corrections on visuals, sort out practical and technical snags, retime cut scripts, and cut more if necessary.

6. *The Run-through*

Everybody who has been involved in the presentation should come to the run-through. By now most of the practical and technical problems should be sorted out, and everyone can see for the first time something close to what the audience will see. Not much can be done now in the way of alterations and embellishments, but it is still possible to cut. It can be painful to do so this late, when so much care and trouble has been put in; nevertheless, it is the ability to cut at this stage, even to cut a complete address, that sorts out the men from the boys.

7. *The Dress Rehearsal*

The dress rehearsal is different from the run-through in that it is held in the actual location where the presentation is to be given, with all the attendant facilities and circumstances as close as possible to what they will be on the day of the presentation. The purpose of this is to try and reveal any special snags that could not be foreseen, and to give the presenters some territorial familiarity to diminish their apprehensions.

Action. Cross fingers.

5 / Delivery
and the Use of Words

Should the presenter have a written script, or just talk more or less spontaneously from a few notes? This is a constantly recurring question, and one to which more people come up with the wrong answer than any other.

To start with, let us all agree that the best talker is the most natural. He is easy, fluent, friendly, amusing, and free from the fetters that seem to bind others to small pieces of paper. He is just talking to us in the most natural way in the world: no script for him—how could there be? He is talking only to us, and basing what he says on our reactions as he goes along. Such a talk cannot by definition be scripted.

The Problems of Unscripted Presentation

For most of us, however, an unscripted presentation is an aspiration rather than a description. Our tongues are not so honeyed; our words are less winged. And even for those who can on occasions touch those heights, there are three difficulties.

1. Visuals. A brilliant talker does not need visual aids to keep the audience from falling asleep, but the subject of a presentation very often demands these aids. And if you have them, it can be fatal to depart from the prepared order in which they are to appear. The slides and flip charts are in a prearranged sequence; the operator has a fixed point at which to leave the slide machine and go to the film projector; and a brilliant extempore performance will mess the whole thing up.

2. Time. A presentation is almost always limited in time, and a certain amount has to be said in that time. Without fairly careful scripting, time is likely to be wildly overrun, or important points may be omitted.

3. The best way. If you accept the fact that certain points have to be made in a certain time to a certain audience, the logic of optimization takes over. There is a best order in which to make the points. There is a best way of putting them across to make them clear to the audience. There are best words and phrases to emphasize your arguments. Quite soon you discover that any genuinely spontaneous performance is not practicable, so it might as well all be scripted.

Most people get to this stage, and this is where it all goes wrong. They sit down at their desk, write out what they want to say, hand it to their secretary, and tell themselves that they have written their presentation. But they haven't. They have written a paper.

Don't Read a Paper

I am not sure why it is slightly offensive and insulting to have a document read to you, or obviously memorized and recited to you, in this sort of situation. Eminent professors read papers to learned societies, and no one complains. But in those cases the audience are usually receiving (or hope they are receiving) a privileged preview of a new contribution to knowledge which will later be published. I think it is partly because a presentation is usually to some extent a favor bestowed by those who attend on those who present. If it is all written out, why bother to make the journey and take up all this time? Why not just put the document in the mail? Reading or memorizing is also an insult to the individuality of the audience; if they have taken the trouble to come, they expect to be talked to as themselves, whereas a written document has obviously been completed before its author ever encountered them, and can obviously be delivered by any speaker to any audience. Indeed the larger the audience, the less offensive it becomes (though it is never elegant). But when the audience is under a hundred, as most presentation audiences are, reading a paper can be sufficiently irritating to defeat the purpose of the presentation. Certainly the encyclopedia salesman who called on my wife and me one evening and proceeded to recite his company's official spiel at us, word for word, as if he were chatting, gave the most powerful impression of fraudulent insincerity that I have ever witnessed in my own drawing room (at least when the television was off).

So it seems that if you read your script you are insulting and if you learn it and recite it you are insincere. What is the answer?

Spoken English and Written English

The answer lies in the difference between written and spoken English. If you write out a script and practice it enough, you will know it pretty well by heart when the time comes; but if what you started from was written English, then it will still sound like a memorized document. If what you started from was spoken English, it will sound like an informal talk.

It is worth taking a little time to talk about the difference between the two kinds of language, because if you can see the difference and avoid the pitfalls it makes a tremendous improvement on your sense of ease and relaxation, and helps you to avoid the barrier which so many speakers unwittingly construct between themselves and their audience. What is more, it is perfectly possible to sit down at your desk and write spoken English—professional broadcasters do it all the time. You just have to be aware of what it involves.

Writing spoken English. First of all, the spoken language has its roots not in literature or newspapers or memos or any printed page, but in the un-self-conscious speech of ordinary people. When writing written English you ask yourself if what you have written is clear and grammatical and concise. With spoken English, it has to go through another filter as well: Is it the sort of thing someone might actually say to someone else? Or to be more precise, is there anything in it that no one could possibly say to anyone else? On the printed page you may get away with the word "for" meaning "because," but in speech you simply can't say "I must get some flowers, for it's my wife's birthday." On the printed page people may wed after gem raids, but in speech they get married after jewel robberies; in speech a group of three is not *a*, *b*, and *c*, but *a* and *b* and *c*. Anything that smacks of journalese or archaism or purple prose or literariness is a bar to communication—as a member of the audience you instantly feel "Whoever this chap is talking to, it isn't me." This doesn't mean everything has to be at the level of chit chat—on the contrary, part of the craft consists in writing carefully and well while the audience just feel they are being talked to by an interesting person.

In fact writing good spoken English may mean writing ungrammatically. Grammatically correct English can be bad spoken English; just count how many times anyone says the word "whom" to you tomorrow. Few people can say "For whom are you doing it?" and get away with it. "Who are you doing it for?" may be bad grammar, but in a presentation it's the only way. And of course you can cash in on the vernacular. You might write "A million dollars for a national theater may sound like a lot of money, but compared with the defense budget it's a drop in the ocean." You can say "compared with the defense budget, it's peanuts" and make your point a good deal more vigorously. Slang always gets a license to operate in the vernacular long before it's allowed out on the printed page without the use of quotation marks. And with spoken English you can use the first and second person where the more formal written English would use the third: not "The user will have encountered similar examples of failures of domestic equipment which can be exasperating even if not dangerous" but "I expect you know the sort of thing I mean—the gadget that wakes you up with a hot cup of tea at three in the morning, the vacuum cleaner that blows when it ought to suck. Even when it's harmless it's the kind of thing that drives me up the wall—and it's not always harmless." Incidentally no respectable writer of written English would put "sort of thing" and "kind of thing" so close to each other on a printed page, but in spoken English it passes unnoticed.

So much for the first and greatest difference. The source is the spoken language, not the written language. You must never make yourself say anything that would sound oddly formal, stilted, or literary if used in ordinary conversation. Incidentally, you also have to be careful with words that sound the same—remember that size may mean stature or it may mean windy suspirations, and the audience haven't got the spelling to help them.

Word order and signposting. The second fundamental difference is that when reading the written word you can go at your own pace; you can pause to reflect, or to consult a dictionary or the *Oxford Companion to English Literature.* You can go back and read the beginning of the sentence or the chapter or article again. If it is so written that you are obliged to, it is probably not very well written, but you can make it out in the end. But the spoken word comes at you down a single line, as it were. You can never look on to the end of a sentence or back to the start of it. You can't stop it for a second, you can't make it go more slowly. And so in writing for that sort of communication you have to think in a new way about clarity and lucidity. In a presentation you not only have to present all the relevant information clearly, but you have to present it in the best order for assimilation. For instance if you say "Dickens, Socrates, Drake, Lincoln, Henry VIII—they all had beards," you don't say why all the names are being mentioned till the last word of the sentence. When it comes, you are asking the audience to go back and mentally draw beards on all five men—if they can remember who they were. If you say "Dickens had a beard; so did Socrates, Drake, Lincoln, and Henry VIII," you are drawing the beards on each one. I'm not saying you can't ask them to make this mental effort, only that you must be aware you are demanding it. Similarly if a man tells you, "In the last year Harry Smith has climbed the Matterhorn, swum the Hellespont, crossed the Sahara, run from London to Brighton, shot Niagara Falls in a canoe, and did all this while blindfolded and with one hand tied behind his back," he may get a certain shock effect, but he is asking you to go back and do all those things again in your head in the light of this new information.

Also the audience has no paragraphing to guide them; you must allow for this too. The device is known as "signposting." You may know you've reached the end of one idea and are on to the next; they don't. So for the spoken language much more than for the written you have to draw the threads together, summarize where you've got to, and indicate where you're going next. "So there was Ulysses, imprisoned inside the cyclops's cave with his crew. How was he going to get out? Well, every morning . . ." Homer did it more gracefully, but he still had to do it—he too was writing for live audiences rather than readers.

Plant your facts. The rhetorical question also has an important function in arranging the order in which you present information. You must have noticed that it's much easier to assimilate a fact if you've wanted to know it rather than if it's just presented to you. The rhetorical question is a good way of digging a hole to plant a fact in. I first learned this by seeing it done wrong on television. There was a film reconstructing Hannibal's route across the Alps. The commentary said "That flat rock is probably where Hannibal spent the third night, because Livy says they only made five miles on the third day and Polybius says they camped on a high flat rock." How much better to say "Now we had to work out where they spent the third night. Well, it must have been near here because Livy says they only made five miles on the third day. Polybius said it was on a high flat rock." By that time everyone is looking for the rock anyway, and they probably spot it first.

You also have to be very careful with the involved sentence culminating in the main verb. It is supposed to be bad literary style to write a sentence that has various grammatical ending places before the full stop—the sort of sentence where you can go on chopping pieces off the end without necessitating syntactic change. But it's usually good spoken English writing, for two reasons. Listen to this literary version: "Whatever the works manager says, if the financial projections look right and the market tests are encouraging, at least in the capital goods business, it's usually safe to authorize a development budget." In the first place you have to store all those parentheses in your head till you know what the speaker and the works manager were arguing about; in the second place it is the opposite from the way people talk. In ordinary speech the main thoughts nearly always come first, or near the beginning. "Whatever the works manager says, it's usually safe to authorize a development budget, at least in the capital goods business, as long as the financial projections look right and the market tests are encouraging." So on the whole, it's better to put your parentheses after the main verb, and it's a bad idea to pile several up before it. And of course short sentences are better than long ones—though this isn't different from written English.

Avoid abstract nouns. There is another principle of spoken English which is also true of written English, but even more important with an audience who cannot stop and puzzle a sentence out: the avoidance of abstract nouns. They are the barbiturates of communication: soporific in small doses and lethal in large ones. A steady and sober citizen who will tell you privately "We'll make sure you can hear it properly" will write "We will give special attention to the provision of adequate sound reception facilities." He might even write "The consequence of your interposition of a manual obstruction on my area of locution is the inhibition of communication" when he would say "If you put your hand over my mouth, I can't talk." A total ban on the use of abstract nouns, despite the restrictions it imposes, would have made a net overall improvement on nearly all the presentations I have attended. The aim of all writing, according to Robert Louis Stevenson, is to affect your reader precisely as you wish. This is equally true of writing spoken English, and the word "precisely" is the key: The concrete noun is a precision tool, and the abstract noun a blunt instrument.

Use examples and analogies. Perhaps this is the point to advocate the use of analogy. A well-chosen parallel from within the audience's experience is often more valuable than a hundred dollars' worth of visual aids or ten minutes of involved explanation. I only started to understand what computer software was when someone presented me with this analogy: "Compare it with your secretary. Her value depends on three factors: (1) her general intelligence and suitability for the job, (2) her training—arithmetic, English, languages, shorthand, typing, bookkeeping, and so on, and (3) how well she knows and carries out the specific jobs of your office and your firm. Well, (1) is the basic design and circuitry of the computer—like intelligence, there's not much you can do about it now; (2) is the manufacturer's software, supplied by the computer—this includes routines like payroll and invoicing which nearly every user wants from a computer, just as he wants shorthand and typing from a secretary; (3) is the user's own software—the programs special to his own company which he writes for himself, just as you teach the secretary her duties when she joins." That sort of simple and homely parallel may not be a complete explanation, but it is clear and brief, and is ideal for a presentation. If anyone wants to know more, there are lots of books available.

So much for the two main ways in which a presentation script differs from a written paper. It draws on the vocabulary, grammar, and syntax of ordinary speech instead of literary English, and it comes at the viewer down a single line; he can't see what's coming or what's gone, nor can he vary the pace or go back.

Different levels of knowledge. There is one other difference that matters: difference in level of knowledge. Some of your audience are specialist experts, some reasonably well informed, some rather hazy about it all. If you were writing a journal, this wouldn't matter. Some would read it fast, some slowly, some just glance at it. No one would blame you for telling them something they already knew—they bought the journal, and it's their fault if it's too technical or if there's nothing they want to know in it.

But you invited them to the presentation—so, do you explain things carefully for the less expert and bore or even insult the experts, or do you talk to the experts and baffle the nonspecialists (who are probably senior to them)? This in fact is a problem that broadcasters face in an acute form. Suppose for instance you are writing about who will succeed McNamara, and suppose you suspect many of your audience don't know what he does. Do you say "McNamara is president of the World Bank. He used to be the U.S. Secretary of Defense. Before that he was chief executive of Ford. He joined them from the U.S. Air Force after the war." If you do, half the audience decides this is too elementary and so not meant for them. In fact of course you have to use dodges. You say "Robert McNamara's successor must pose a problem. How do you follow a man who learned management techniques in the U.S. Air Force thirty years ago, who went to Ford and rose to chief executive, and then became Secretary of Defense?" You have to find all the possible ways of dropping background facts casually and inoffensively. And you frequently employ such invaluable phrases as "broadly speaking," "for the most part," "in general," "with certain exceptions" to avoid piling up tedious exceptions and qualifications while at the same time showing the experts you know about them. You will also find that the specialist expert will not object to a really good explanation—he may want to use it himself one day. But you have to remember both halves of C. P. Scott's* advice—never overestimate your audience's knowledge; never underestimate their intelligence. I think it is fatal to believe your audience to be less intelligent than you, though it is wise to expect them to be less well informed. Also I ought to make it clear that the principles of good writing still hold for good speaking: compression, lucidity, vividness, force, the avoidance of ambiguity—these are the aims of a presentation script just as much as of writing for the printed page. It is the means of achieving them that are different.

Delivery

The actual delivery of the presentation—elocution and voice production and projection—is not something you can teach in a book; moreover, now that microphones and loudspeakers are so common, it is much less of a critical factor than it used to be. For most presenters,

---

* Scott became famous through his fifty-odd years as editor of the *Manchester Guardian* when he built that publication's great reputation.

*For most presenters, the chief problem
is to overcome speaker's rigidity.*

the chief problem is to overcome speaker's rigidity. You must often have seen how someone who talks in an animated, interesting, and persuasive way suddenly becomes wooden and monotonous when he steps onto a platform to address a couple of dozen people. Some terrible demon of self-consciousness seems to paralyze the muscles of his face and constrict his vocal chords. All I can say is that experience makes this demon depart, but the departure can be delayed by two factors: (1) using written English instead of spoken English and (2) failure to realize that good speaking consists of addressing a large number of people as if they were a single person. The aim, in fact, is to use the same movements of face, head, and body; the same range of vocal pitch and volume; the same gestures; the same pace and pauses as you use when talking to a couple of friends over a drink. But it is not a question of acquiring these characteristics; the task is to remove the barriers which are keeping them back. Anyone who cannot remove them with practice and experience should give up speaking in public or take a public speaking course. However, if you are addressing a thousand people without a microphone, this natural and easy manner is impossible and you are in the world of genuine oratory which is something quite different in technique, even if identical in objective (see Chapter 7).

Mannerisms and Distractions

Presenters can help each other by watching each other for a few common and obvious faults which are hard to notice in oneself. (1) A physical mannerism, such as scratching the ear, is only worth correcting if it is frequent enough to distract the audience so that they are watching for it with greater interest than they are listening to the presentation. (2) Verbal mannerisms, such as the recurring phrases: "The thing is . . . ," "in this connection . . . ," and so on. Again, the same qualification applies as in (1). (3) Turning away or looking down while speaking, so that the end of the sentence is lost. And (4), by far the most important and most common, dropping the voice (in pitch or pitch and volume together, but seldom just volume) at the end of a sentence. Those who do this are usually completely unconscious of it, and it has a most boring and deadening effect. It gives the presentation a finale at the end of every sentence and tells the audience to switch off their receivers. Each new sentence has to make them switch on again. However, once the offender is made aware that he is doing this—by listening to a playback tape, for instance—he is three-quarters of the way to overcoming it.

Note: Written versus Spoken English

As an example of the difference between written and spoken English, I have written the sort of paragraph one encounters all too frequently in management papers and have "translated" it into the language I would use if I were delivering it in a speech or presentation. It is no accident that the spoken version is longer—the vague abstractions of the written version have to be solidified into concrete examples if they are to penetrate the audience's mind through the ear rather than the eye.

WRITTEN ENGLISH

The reader may have noted the tendency to inflation of self-importance on the part of the scientist and development engineer in large corporations. It is the product of a combination of influences—partly the significance accorded to his contribution in the area of his industrial operations, partly a recognition of the distinction accorded to his qualifications in his social and domestic environment. Furthermore his section of the population is given particular prominence in the achievement of the objectives of the nation. There is also the opportunity for building a reputation among professional and academic institutions outside the corporation, in both the national and the international fields. In addition there is the enhancement of the attitude of the scientist as an exception, produced by those with responsibility for the management of the corporation: his nonconformity, unreliability, and intellectual capacity become the subject of their respect and admiration, despite its divergence from their own conscientious normality of behavior. Consequently his occupation is full of temptation toward an arrogant inflation of his own self-esteem.

SPOKEN ENGLISH

Let's imagine a large research and development organization. Suppose it has a hundred scientists working in it—or even two hundred, if you like. And imagine you're one of those scientists—perhaps a development engineer. Quite soon you begin to feel that, if an organization that big relies on you, then you must be quite a guy. And you begin to feel you ought to be treated as quite a guy too. After all, you're pretty well respected at home; the neighbors tell visitors, "He's a scientist" in a reverent sort of voice—the voice their parents would have used to say, "He's a priest." And you've even got a sort of national importance: Don't people in government keep saying how we need more scientists if the economy is to keep growing? But that's not all. You have an existence, an identity, in a world beyond the corporation. You've got links with your old university, and with other universities. You attend scientific congresses at home and abroad. You belong to a brotherhood that's far wider and far more illustrious than the gray organization men who work alongside you. And what's more, they go out of their way to help you feel that you're an exception. They build your myth. They invent stories about your absent-mindedness. They tell each other how you corrected the computer's square roots. Of course they're all sober-suited and clean shaven, and yet if you arrive in a yellow shirt with no jacket and a beard, they're delighted. One way and another, if you're a scientist in industry today, it's quite a struggle *not* to think of yourself as a cut above everyone else.

6 / Visual Aids
and the Use of Pictures

The subject of visual aids and their uses deserves several volumes. To list them all, with their full details and variations, to describe the operation and assess the advantages and disadvantages of each one would require (in Max Beerbohm's phrase) a far less brilliant pen than mine. This chapter deals only with those which are most handy for presentations and is concerned not with the routine uses which most people get right but with the ways in which I have most often seen them misused, messed up, or wasted.

Let us first be clear about the disadvantages of visual aids. They take up a great deal of time and thought; they can divert attention away from what is to be said and on to how it is to be said; they diminish flexibility; they cost money; and, if they go wrong, the result can vary from mild confusion to the ultimate in catastrophe and humiliation. So why do we use them at all?

We use them because a picture is worth a thousand

words, because they can portray vividly and instantly things that are impossible to convey verbally, they save time, they create interest, they bring variety, they add impact, and they remain in the memory long after the words have left it. There is no question that a good presentation which employs visuals is enormously more effective than a good presentation without them. Usually the advantages outweigh the disadvantages, but the disadvantages are there. So the first question to ask about every visual is, "Can we manage just as well without it?" I sometimes suspect that up to one-third of all visuals used in presentations would be excluded by that question. I can hear the poor presenter being asked "Do you want any visual aids?" and being shamed into saying yes for fear of appearing casual or lazy or amateur, and then dreaming up some slides he doesn't want and which don't help.

The second question is "Is this really a visual, or just a visible verbal?" If I could engrave a single sentence on every presenter's heart, it would be this: *Words are not visuals*. How many times have we sat at presentations and seen slide after slide portraying nothing except abstract nouns, such as objectives, operations; preparation, planning, productivity, progress; reconnaissance, recognition, reporting, and so on in an endless and utterly unmemorable series. Words are what the presenter is there for; he is provided with the complex and ingenious equipment of tongue, lips, teeth, pharynx, larynx, and lungs in order to utter them. It is not possible to make a rule banning all words from visual aids, because they are sometimes necessary to help the audience identify pictures, and just occasionally an expert finds ways of using them effectively and dramatically; otherwise it would be an excellent rule.

Is this really a visual, or just a visible verbal?

Those then are the two basic rules, which are very obvious when you state them baldly: A visual must be necessary and it must be visual. In addition, all the individual visual aids in common use have special ways of either tripping presenters up or offering them opportunities which they fail to take. The following paragraphs give the main points to watch.

Blackboard

1. White chalk doesn't show up as well as yellow.
2. Dry duster is not as efficient as damp duster or sponge.
3. Good straight lines, circles, and the like can be achieved by drawing them on the board in pencil before the presentation, then chalking over the pencil line. Audience can't see pencil line and think you are another Giotto.
4. If you are right-handed, board should be on your left as you face the audience, so you obscure much less of it when drawing. If you have room, start drawing one-third of the way across, using only the remaining two-thirds, and you obscure less still.
5. When pointing at the board, stay on the same side and point with your left hand, so that you stay facing the audience.
6. If using a pointer, don't let the point wander vaguely round the board. Point at what you want, leave it there motionless, then take it away.
7. If using a pointer, suppress all impulses to use it as a swagger stick, conductor's baton, backscratcher, or toothpick.
8. If you have to talk while drawing, remember that

by turning round you have suddenly made it twice as hard for the audience to hear you. Better to avoid doing so—or at least avoid confiding in the blackboard.

9. Corollary of (8): Try and plan your use of the blackboard so that you are never drawing for more than a few seconds at a stretch. Even if you only break off for a sentence or two, it's a great deal better.

10. Clear the board as soon as you have finished with what is on it. It's a distraction if you leave up old drawings when you've moved on. Put a spare piece of chalk in your pocket.

11. Check the blackboard in advance for stability of legs and pegs (I would be ashamed to mention anything this elementary if I had not witnessed the consequence of a failure to do so).

Large White Paper Pad and Felt-tipped Pen

A large white paper pad and felt-tipped pen are much like the blackboard in principle, and most of the same rules apply. The chief differences are:

1. Colors are much more effective on white than on black.

2. Because you can't erase, you have to get rid of the previous sheet each time. If the pad is perforated and you just tear off the sheets and drop them, the stage starts to look ridiculous by about the sixth sheet. This can be a slight embarrassment to those who follow. Or will you go down on your hands and knees and pick up the fallen sheets yourself? A decent sized cardboard box is usually the answer. If the sheets fold back at the top, they are liable to start falling back on you after the first six, so rehearse right through.

Flip Charts

Flip charts are a useful aid, but are not used enough.

1. Drawings are too small for the audience to be able to see details. Drawings must be bold and simple.

2. There is the same fold-over problem as with large white paper pads. Ring hinges are the solution.

3. Flip charts are very good (and not sufficiently used) for cartoon illustrations of abstract concepts such as ease of maintenance and maneuverability.

4. As with the others, it can be distracting if a picture is left up after it has served its purpose, but if you fold back to the cover you may have a job finding your place. The answer is to have a neutral interleaf after every picture or picture sequence. (This interleaf doesn't have to be blank—it can be a symbol or picture that is relevant to your whole presentation.)

Build-up Visuals

Build-up visuals include all those visual aids, like magnetic boards, slot boards, and pin boards, that create a total picture by continually adding pictures to a basic design. The simplest and cheapest is one used by the army. Cards are backed with sandpaper and placed on a blanket which is stretched over a blackboard. It works surprisingly well.

The snag here is confusion over the pieces to be added. If you are adding six different types of visual design and you have ten of each, you spend most of the presentation hunting through sixty assorted objects for the one you want. Therefore, the rule must be to use either a very limited number or a very limited range.

The alternative (which solves this problem) is the revelation board, which starts blank or with a simple framework and is progressively revealed by removing blank cards. (This is of course the same basic equipment, but used for subtraction instead of addition.) The snag here is revealing too slowly in the early stages, so that boredom sets in because the audience can see how much further there is to go. You must use a stripper's technique of removing the first coverings fairly quickly: As interest rises you can afford to slow down a little and draw out the suspense.

Physical Objects

In the search for helpful or memorable visual aids, it is all too easy to forget the value of a small object fished out of the pocket or a larger one from under the desk. It is worth making a special effort to think of any object, or part of an object, which could be interesting and reasonably relevant to display. Because the presenters are familiar with printed circuits or the inside of film cassettes or computer storage discs, they forget that their audience have quite possibly never seen one. Simply producing one and holding it up turns an abstract idea into a physical object, causes virtually no delay, and substitutes a memorable picture for a forgettable word. If you have enough of each object to pass around to the audience, better still.

One of the most memorable instances of solid objects being used in this way was demonstrated in England just after transistors had been developed. British engineers and physicists were desperately and fruitlessly trying to get hold of them for examination and experimentation when an American came over to address a learned society about them. At one point he said, "Anybody want to take one home?" To the audience's disbelieving gasp, he fished in his pocket and brought out a great handful of transistors and just threw them into the audience. The effect, I am told, was like throwing a handful of rice to a mob of starving refugees. Distinguished professors groveled and fought on their hands and knees; there was pushing and clawing and stamping on fingers and cries of pain or accusation; and it was minutes before the flushed and flustered gathering returned to their seats clutching their booty. Only then did the lecturer say, "It's all right, they're all duds."

Working Models

The successful use of a working model is usually the high point of a presentation—ask any science master. If it fails to work, it is almost always a major disaster. This however is not an argument against the use of working demonstrations, only a plea for the most extreme care in preparation and rehearsal, and also (where possible) a standby equally well tested and prepared. Those who are to participate in the demonstration should practice and practice until boredom sets in, and for this almost more than anything else the actual location of the presentation should be checked for power supply, ventilation, fire regulations, or anything else that could throw everything out at the last minute.

Overhead Projector

By an overhead projector, I mean the sort operated by the presenter. For some reason they rarely work as well in presentations as they do in classrooms. The reason,

I think, is that they take too much of the presenter's mind away from his audience. He has to worry about getting his plates in the right order, about getting them the right way up and the right way round; he has to keep checking the screen behind him; and the effect is too often cumbersome, didactic, and slow. To be successful, they need a lot of care in rehearsal and restraint in use; they should not be required to do as much as they technically can. The presenter must become so familiar with the equipment that he can use it casually.

Slides

Of all the available visual aids, I can think of none that are used more frequently or more ineptly than slides. They are very valuable but they can be great destroyers of presentations. Give slide projectors the care and respect you would give a loaded pistol. Their faults are of two kinds, conceptual and operational, but of course they can compound each other and all too often they do. By conceptual faults I mean inadequate thought from the point of view of the audience. The seven chief conceptual errors are:

1. Too verbal. I have mentioned this fault earlier in the chapter, but it is worth mentioning again here because it seems to be slides that are the chosen vehicle for those who think words are pictures. Discipline yourself to ask "What will this slide *show?*" and never "What will this slide *say?*"

2. Too comprehensive. Technical people are especially prone to the vice of insisting that every nut and bolt be included in the slide. Remember that a slide is only a part of what you are asking the audience to take in—you supply the other part with what you say over it. You can always say "This of course is only a broad outline of the system," "This is an extreme simplification—the full plan is in your folder," and so on. Indeed the best slides are not sufficient on their own; they need the presenter's words to make them properly intelligible. If they don't, the audience is liable to stop listening to him and start working out the information on the slide.

3. *Too complex.* Many slides are such a mass of boxes and arrows and feedback control loops that you might as well put up a maze from a comic book ("How can Teddy get back to his home without crossing any lines?"). This, even more than the slide that is too comprehensive, distracts the audience from anything you have to say unless you work through it laboriously—and even then you will be too quick for some or too slow for others, or both. The solution is usually to break it down into a sequence of successive slides—indeed this simple dodge on its own would have redeemed something like a third of the communication failures I have witnessed in slide presentations.

4. *Too crowded.* Jamming too much onto a slide, even if reasonably simple, makes it impossible for the back half of the audience to see important details. If in any doubt, get someone *who has never seen the slide before* to sit at the furthest audience distance and be honest. If you try it yourself an insidious optimism provides false reassurance. Again the solution is almost always the same as in paragraph 3—a sequence of slides instead of just one.

5. *Too colorless.* Far too many black lines on clear slides make the slides appear colorless. Apart from the pleasant variation that colors give, once you start thinking in terms of a color range you begin to find ways in which color keys and codes can be used to help the audience's comprehension by giving additional information.

6. *Held too long.* Once a slide has made its point it should be removed unless there is a positive reason for keeping it there. Otherwise it becomes a distraction.

7. *Not explained.* I find it quite incredible how often a presenter puts up a slide—usually an extremely complex and comprehensive slide—and continues talking with only the faintest reference to it, leaving the audience with two or three minutes of quite hard work puzzling it out before they are free to start listening to him again. I suppose it is because the slide is so familiar to him by then that he assumes it is familiar to the audience too. Or else it is some strange ritual homage to the vampire-goddess Video. It seems blindingly obvious to urge presenters to work through their slides with the audience if they have any elucidatory or corroborative purpose at all, but from my experience it is important advice.

So much for the main faults in terms of the content of slides. All of them are barriers to communication. The operational faults however provoke something much more damaging—ridicule. When the third slide comes on upside down, even the most polite audience are starting to laugh. After the fifth, there isn't a dry seat in the house. However much people may sympathize, each one of them takes away a private conviction that you're not to be trusted with hanging up a picture, let alone carrying out a five million dollar aerospace contract. Most of the problems center on either the projector or the projectionist.

The projector. Consider the manufacturer's problem. His machine is electrical in power, mechanical in operation, and hot all the time it is running. It must be light and portable, but strong and resistant to bangs, bashes, and to being dropped on the floor. It must be easily operated even by buffoons. Purchasers expect it to be cheap and to run efficiently and without maintenance for upwards of thirty-five years.

Now read the preceding paragraph again.

Right? Then I hope you have made the necessary deduction. *You must assume the projector is going to go wrong.* In fact I am constantly surprised that they do not go wrong more often, but they go wrong enough. It is not disastrous if you are prepared for it (standby projector, vital pictures also on flip chart, contingency plans thought out), but if you have assumed the projector will not go wrong and also hinged your presentation on it, you deserve all you get. And always try out all the slides in advance on the projector you will actually be using, if possible in the place where you will be using it. Your slides may be the wrong size, the heat of the arc may burn them—you never know till you try.

The projectionist. You may have one of those projectors which you operate yourself by pressing a button. They have a great advantage, which is unified control. You yourself load the slides, you yourself project them. For small audiences they are the safest, but usually their throw is too short to give a large enough picture for a big audience. Then you are up against the projectionist problem, the problem of divided control.

If you think slide projectionist is just another technical job like house electrician, I have to assume that you have never given a presentation that included a slide sequence. Technical proficiency is only a very small part of the job. It chiefly requires intelligence, initiative, coolness of head, and presence of mind. The projectionist must have a thorough knowledge of, and familiarity with, the script. He must be alert for every accidental change of order, and be ready to rearrange his slides accordingly. He must be incapable of confusing the signal "next slide" with the signal "remove this slide." And of course he must never put a slide inside out or upside down, and never throw the next trayload on the floor as he is about to reload.

For all these reasons, the presenter's understudy, if he has one, is the person to operate the projector. But whoever the understudy is, I suggest the following procedure for the presenter and the projectionist:

• They should go through the slides by hand against the script and then, having loaded them, go through them with the script twice.

• They must never make any cuts or order changes after their final rehearsal.

• They should try and avoid reloads during the presentation (second magazine or second projector).

• If a slide is required twice they should make two copies, never try to lift it out and insert it in a different place.

• The projectionist must have a flashlight to find fallen slides under seats.

• They should agree to a breakdown procedure. For example, if a slide sticks, do they drop it or try and return to it?

One final point: You may be provided with a powerful flashlight whose beam projects a small bright arrow onto the screen to identify points on slides. *Do not use it.* It is nearly always a distraction, both to the speaker who has to aim it and find his target and to the audience as it wanders around the screen like Tinkerbell in Peter Pan. It has a use, but a highly specialized one: It is useful for identifying obscure details in actuality slides (landscapes, X rays, news photographs) when the screen is too large or too distant for the speaker to use a pointer. Any slide you design yourself should be designed to be clear without it, and nearly all others you will be able to identify quite satisfactorily either verbally or with a pointer.

If all these warnings are heeded and all the precautions are taken, slides on their own can turn a pedestrian talk into a competent presentation. But they can also turn a man into a monkey.

Tape Recordings

Aural rather than visual aids are not often called on, but it is worth considering whether some noise or music or spontaneous dialogue might help. But tape recordings can be offensive to use for messages from members of your own organization who might have come in person.

Cassette Film Projectors

Cassette film projectors are a fairly new development and an extremely valuable one, especially those which have synchronous sound. But they are only suitable for quite small numbers. On the other hand they are much easier to stop and start than a proper film projector.

Film

A good synchronous sound film is the surest and most complete presentation in itself. However a film made for a different purpose but included in your presentation needs special care.

1. Be careful not to run any section for too long. After a while it starts to take over and becomes the presentation, diminishing the importance and impact of everything else.

2. Resist the temptation of using a good bit of film just because it's good. Discipline yourself to reject it unless you can make it relevant. People remember good film, and you don't want their vividest memory to be of something irrelevant.

3. Remember that film is for *moving* pictures; it is to show things that move. Don't commission film when still pictures would do the job better as well as more cheaply.

4. Space your film carefully throughout the presentation for maximum effect.

5. Be very careful of commenting live over silent film. Once the film has started it is more or less inexorable; if you have a sneezing fit, the pictures will go on changing at the same rate (unlike slides). You may get behind and be unable to catch up or find your place. If you do decide to risk it, at least have plenty of rehearsal with the picture and get to know it well with special attention to the points at which the picture is about to change to something else. Otherwise you find yourself talking about a picture that is not there, and failing to explain the one that is.

There is an enormous amount to say about the actual making of documentary film, but it is beyond the scope of this book. However some people who are not film makers sometimes find themselves faced with the necessity of writing the commentary on a film. This is a highly specialized craft, but it is possible to give certain basic guidelines; these are provided in Chapter 10.

Giant Screen Television (Eidophor)

If you can afford it, a giant screen television (an eidophor) can bring into a presentation live pictures of what is actually going on at the moment in factories, laboratories, stores, docks, refineries, and the like all over the country, or indeed all round the world. However it presents the complexities of a major television program and needs professional help from the start. More simply, it can be used just in the venue of the presentation to enlarge for a big audience a demonstration of something detailed—the action of a small motor, a computer printing out—when the "liveness" is too important to make film the answer.

There is however a further possible use, and one which requires much more careful consideration: This is to point the camera at the speaker and throw his vastly enlarged picture onto the screen. It sounds like an excellent idea, but it carries with it a very grave danger. At the root of a good presentation lies the speaker-audience relationship (see Chapter 7). By turning the speaker into a television relay picture you can destroy that relationship and reduce the audience, who are a kind of participant while the occasion is them-plus-the-speaker, into passive *dégagé* spectators. This is emphasized when the speaker is moved to the side of the stage to give a clear view of the screen, and when the camera is placed between him and the audience for a full-face picture.

On the whole, therefore, it is a temptation which should be resisted. Only with an extremely large audience should it be considered at all, because then the advantages for the people at the back are much larger and the disadvantages smaller. If it is used in such a case, the camera should be well back in the auditorium on a long focus lens, so that the presenter is in direct touch with most of his audience with the camera simply observing him. The screen should be placed halfway back down the auditorium so that the front few hundred cannot see it and will consequently participate in the live presentation while the back ones, who would have been rather out of it otherwise, at least get a good view.

Videotape and Television Production

Small television cameras with microphones, tape recording units, and monitor screens can now be bought for a few hundred dollars. Unfortunately the skills of television production are not so easily or cheaply acquired. Although the potential benefits of such equipment are obviously large, I would advise extreme caution until quite a lot of experience has been built up.

Obviously you can use the transmitting part of the equipment for purchased tapes or transferred film. It is the use of the recording part, the camera, that needs care. As long as it is simply pointed at places and objects and machines it will do no harm—the trouble starts when it is pointed at people. Every television producer knows the danger: The whole world has no sight to offer that is as spellbinding and satisfying as yourself talking on a television screen. Most people do it very badly (the natural ease of the television professional is a skilled technique that requires training and practice), but are undeterred. A few learn to do it better, and become inordinately pleased with themselves. All of them talk about it with great modesty ("I don't really know if it comes off—Oh, do you think so?") but they soon get hooked; they'd always thought they could do it better than those telly boys if only they got the chance. Now they've got it. You will never persuade the chairman that there is even a second of boredom for the audience in a forty-five minute medium close-up of him saying what a fine future the company has if only everyone gets down to it and pulls together. Indeed if you work for him, it would be unwise to try. And so the danger of this equipment is that it will be used for interminable and counter-productive harangues by senior executives unleashing their egos in the name of internal communications. Even Narcissus couldn't wrap up his reflection on a spool and circulate it around Olympus for transmission with synchronous sound.

Having said all that, I have to admit again that the potential of this equipment as a management aid is very great if it is properly used. But to discuss its proper use would involve the fundamentals of television production, theory, and practice, which like film-making techniques are beyond the scope of this book. For presentations, the camera should be regarded just as a means of collecting visual material that cannot be as well presented in any other way (slide, film, model, and so on), and the monitor screen as a variant of the small cassette film projector. If despite all your efforts you cannot keep people off the screen, try and persuade them to give some point to their use of the medium by doing what is impossible in letter, memo, circular, or tape recorder; that is, sketching, handling a piece of machinery, showing new designs, pointing to particular details on a chart or diagram or balance sheet—any of these help to give a semblance of validity to what may otherwise appear to the recipient as naked and shameless self-glorification or indecent exposure of the ego.

Visual Aids—A Means, Not an End

The final message of this chapter must be the same as the first: Visual aids are a means and not an end. Never include them for their own sake, and always be alert to the damage they can do. Never take great leaps into the dark with technical equipment—increase the complexity, if you must, very gradually. Always choose the less complicated of two kinds of visual aid if there is not much in it. And if you want a motto, the best one is "Keep it simple."

7 / The Audience

| once asked the French singer Juliette Greco about her attitude to a theater full of people who had come to hear her sing. She replied "I try and turn them all into one man—then I try to make him love me. If I can't, I go home." I offer this not as advice to presenters—indeed it is not only impracticable but also probably most inappropriate—but as an insight into the nature of an audience from one of the world's experts in manipulating them. The great paradox of audiences is that the larger they are, the more they become one man. Instead of becoming more diverse, they become more homogeneous. For the presenter there is an additional problem with increasing audience size: The larger the audience, the less they are reacting to what is being presented and the more to the man (or woman) who is presenting it.

So far in this book I have tried to be logical and practical, and restrict myself to principles, practices, and techniques. But I cannot properly explain what I believe to be the essential nature and function of the audience without becoming, if only briefly, theoretical and speculative.

I do not think it matters very much if my theories and speculations are wrong, so long as they help to convey more clearly the deductions I have made after many observations and much thought.

Audiences and Group Behavior

It is becoming more and more widely accepted that much of the behavior of modern man is rooted in the prehistory of our species and of earlier ancestral species. Defense of territory and young, aggression, drives toward status and dominance, exploration, submissive behavior—we exhibit all these characteristics today because they helped our species to survive in the past, and our predecessors who lacked them failed for that reason to become our ancestors. Having for many years sat in audiences; addressed audiences; devised, produced, and written television programs for studio audiences, I am convinced that audiences are a modern expression of a primitive form of group behavior which had survival value in the fairly distant past.

Just what that survival value was, we can only guess. But to me it appears that a large crowd of people packed together in one place achieves two important results that still cannot be so well achieved by any other means: (1) the affirmation of unity and solidarity and (2) the acclamation of leadership. This is not true of small gatherings, but as the audiences grow larger it becomes more and more true. A really large audience is not, for most practical purposes, a place for detailed and reasoned argument. The more people there are, the smaller the proportion whose knowledge, experience, intelligence, and interest are at the right level, and the harder it is

Much of the behavior of modern man is rooted in the prehistory of our species and of earlier ancestral species.

for the argument to be comprehensible and relevant to any but a few. So you have to appeal not to the diverse minds but to the common emotions—hopes and fears, elation and aggression, admiration and contempt, shared experiences and shared aspirations. When you get so many people together, you are not dealing with the intellectual differences of the individual but with the biological identity of the species.

In an audience, we discover our group identity and we accord special prominence and respect to those who lead us to the discovery. It is not an occasion for new ideas, it is a place for demonstrating which ideas the group accepts *as a group,* for affirming the group standards of conduct, for publicly identifying threats to the group, for proclaiming a shared resolve to march forward into the broad sunlit uplands, and for acclaiming those who will lead us to them. It is the political party convention, the strike rally in the docks, the revivalist meeting, the colonel addressing the whole regiment before battle. It is a lot of people crowded together and one man standing above them all. In its most basic form it is the stand-up comedian making us laugh (an aggressive act) at any behavior or idea that we recognize as alien to our group—though this is too complex an idea to pursue here. My guess is that its survival value lies in its power to get several hundred people to act in unison, with a common objective, and under a common leadership. Tribes or troops that could only bind together sixty or seventy would be "evolved out" over a hundred millenia or so of conflict with the larger groupings. That however is a pure guess, and does not affect the argument; it is a deduction, not a premise.

So when is an audience not an audience? In a television studio where laughter is required, most people feel uneasy about laughing until the number of people in the audience climbs above two hundred. A burst of laughter is a good measure of whether a group of people has turned into an audience, but there is no absolute number for it. It depends on whether they are jammed together or scattered thinly around, on how well they knew each other before (jolly coach parties, or just individual couples arriving independently), on whether they have seen the performer before and how often, on whether the auditorium is high and light or low and dark, on the distance between the performer and the front row. Sixty people jammed into a tiny basement night club can be an audience, six hundred dotted around Madison Square Garden can fail to become one.

I have dwelt on this at some length because it is of the most profound importance to presentations. If you have a full audience, you plan and execute differently in all sorts of ways.

What Kind of Audience Will You Have?

The great majority of presentations, in my experience, are not to full audiences. But presentations to full audiences are nearly always very important—even if the presenters do not realize it. But how do you tell if you have a presentation group or a full audience?

Before the arrival of the microphone it was easy. So long as you could reach everyone by talking in your normal voice, it was (and is) an ordinary group. But there comes a time when you have to raise your voice beyond the point where normal speech patterns can be retained. You have to shout, to declaim, to become an orator; if you don't, no one beyond the twelfth row will hear you.

This starts to affect what you can say. You can still cry "Shall we stand idly by when a crisis threatens all we believe in and strive for? Shall we let these unscrupulous villains . . . ?" and so on. It is much harder to shout to a thousand people "So let us bisect the angle ACB with a line CX and produce it until it reaches the circumference at point Y where we will construct a tangent . . ." All very sound stuff, but somehow not worth shouting about. The trouble with the microphone is that it enables speakers to address five hundred people as if they were fifty, and the result is nearly always flat and disappointing. It is usually wise to try and reach the whole audience with the unaided voice, and look upon the microphone just as insurance.

There is no point in going into any further detail about the point of division and demarcation between the two kinds of audience. There is obviously a broad overlap. What matters is to realize that there are two very different kinds of audience, one of fewer than fifty and one of more than two hundred, and that there is an indeterminate area in the middle. For the purposes of this book I have had the small-group audience in my mind, although virtually all I have said holds equally true for a large audience. The purpose of this chapter is to emphasize that if the audience starts to creep up to and over a hundred or so, you have to start thinking very carefully.

What Size Audience Do You Want?

The first question to ask yourself is whether you do in fact want a large audience. Are you, for instance, trying to persuade small groups of decision makers (small) or a large body of decision accepters (large)? Is your real purpose to affirm the unity and raise the morale of a large number of people (large) or to influence the attitudes, ideas, and intentions of a few important people not under your authority (small)? It is not a question of whether you are trying to persuade or not. All public speaking and indeed all writing is one form of persuasion or another.

There is only one area of publication in which men proceed by remorselessly logical steps from unquestionable premises to unarguable conclusions, and it is called science. The beauty of science, and in particular of mathematics, is that you can convince without having to persuade. But in all other areas, persuasion is necessary; our question is simply about the means we use. If a large audience is the best means, assemble one. Book a big hall and send invitations one or two further levels of management down the hierarchy. If a small group is the best means, and three hundred people want to come, hold five sessions during the day or on consecutive days (and remember that they are likely to improve as time goes on, so the last will probably be the most effective). In the no man's land between fifty and two hundred you can have some influence by making the audience compact or scattered, by having house lights on or off, and most of all by the manner of the presenter (for example, formal or relaxed, standing at lectern or sitting on table edge).

The Speakers Must Be Good Enough

If you do want a large audience, you have another question. Are you a good enough speaker? If there are several speakers, are they all good enough? It is not sufficient that they should be capable of addressing small groups—this is one whole grade higher in its demands, and you need speakers who have graduated or who you are sure have the ability to graduate. A speaker who fails with a large audience, especially if he antagonizes them, does himself a great deal of harm. He passes into the folklore of the whole community as a bore or a buffoon or a villain. If all the speakers fail, the cause is lost. This is equally true, of course, of small-group presentations, though the skills are more easily acquired.

All the same, those who lack them should never be allowed to give any presentation of importance however expert or senior they may be. It may sound ridiculous to suggest that important decisions can hang on whether an audience likes a chap or not—and certainly they will never admit it—but very often this is what turns the tide. I am talking about narrow decisions—not whether the airline needs new aircraft, but whose aircraft it should buy. The discussion will be about maintenance and range and consumption and passenger appeal and financial terms and costs and price, and if one plane is clearly superior to its rivals that will be that.

But usually it is not so clear as that, and then the irrational starts to take over the rational, feelings take over arguments, emotion takes over logic. People still talk about objective criteria—costs and consumption and maintenance—but they now use them not to reach rational conclusions but to reinforce irrational ones. Up until the presentation the common ground will have been knowledge of the business and experience and so on. The presentation often gives an extra ingredient for further decision making—a shared feeling among the members of the audience about the kind of person who is trying to persuade them. People will have had private feelings before, but the presentation gives them shared ones. The more airline people who attend, the stronger this will be (for better or worse). There will be a sort of consensus

("Bright bunch, aren't they?" "They really know what they're up to," "Didn't miss a trick"; or else "Somehow I have my doubts about them," "Sure they're building a good aircraft—but are they building it for us?") which becomes a much bigger factor than anyone will admit, and it is based very largely on the impression a few people made on a few other people in the course of a presentation.

I keep hearing about decisions made after totally unemotional logical discussion based exclusively on objective facts, but only in management books. Most narrow decisions, I am convinced, come down more often than anyone yet accepts to primitive tribal acclamation, to a man or a small group of men winning the confidence and respect of another group. I do not even think it wrong that it should be so—very often this is in fact the most important remaining consideration. But we are taking a great risk if we are not aware of it when we are casting our presentations. I doubt if an unsuitable group can effectively persuade their audience that they are suitable, but I have no doubt at all that a suitable one can in the course of a presentation convince them that they are unsuitable.

Pitfalls for Good Speakers

Apart from general incompetence of the kind the earlier chapters are directed at eradicating, there are two faults that most often beset otherwise good speakers. The first is unintentional arrogance. A presentation speaker is usually in an odd position. He is raised up on a platform alone, whereas his superiors in status are shoved together in a group to listen to him. He has this position because of his acknowledged authority on his own subject. The danger comes if he goes outside this authority and begins to make assertions (even if correct) on subjects the audience believe they know more about. By using his special position for this purpose, he is claiming superior status to them not in his own subject (which they concede) but in theirs (which is offensive and insulting). A presenter of an aircraft must not therefore say to the airline "The future of the airline business is for more and more small planes on short routes and fewer but larger on trunk routes." He will employ the formulas of deference and submission and say, "It's not for me to tell you about the future pattern of airline business, but I understand from your own experts that you are expecting . . ."

The second fault (not unconnected) is to wrestle when he should use judo. A presentation is very rarely the time to show people that their strongly held beliefs are erroneous. The most you can do is accept their beliefs but show that they have drawn wrong conclusions. Intellectual judo is using the force of the other man's opinions and prejudices to win your argument. If you try and meet them head on you will not only lose, but risk antagonizing him at the same time. To reiterate the point made earlier, you have to get inside his mind at the planning stage and build your presentation on the foundation of his knowledge, prejudices, attitudes, experience, and needs. If you spend all the time knocking away foundations, you won't build anything at all.

Questions from the Audience

There is one small but important technical point: Should there be questions from the audience? The following guidelines may be helpful:

Size of audience. The larger the audience, the more inhibiting it is to questioners. They feel "Why me and not one of the 799 others?" and "My questions are relevant to only 10 percent of this audience." With very large audiences, up in the hundreds, questions are rarely a good idea.

Can they be damaging? If you suspect that some, or any, of the audience are out to damage you, it is foolish to offer them the opportunity to do it publicly. It is perfectly reasonable to offer to answer questions individually and informally after the presentation.

Can they help? Are the audience likely to feel they are being steamrollered with a sales talk? If there is a danger of this, they should be allowed a chance to say something before the feeling begins to grow. Are you worried that you may be slightly out of touch with their attitude or interests or level of comprehension? If so, their questions may give you valuable guidance.

When should questions be taken? Questions should be asked, in principle, after each discrete section that may generate them. If they are to be helpful, the sooner the better. Also, questions are a useful texture variant (see Chapter 3). The golden rule is that if you have any fears about questions, you should answer questions individually after the session and not during it. Their power to help a presentation is less than their power to damage it.

One-Man Presentation

Finally, we come to the very small presentation. So far in this chapter I have talked about two typical kinds of audience—the audience of less than fifty and the

audience of more than two hundred. There is of course
a third kind, the very small audience of about half a
dozen, usually invited and addressed by a single presenter. Probably this is the most common kind of all,
and it needs to be discussed separately.

The important point about a group of five or six is
that it is not an audience at all. There is no question
of individual identity merging into a single anonymous
unit. Just as it is clear that with six hundred other people
in a hall you cannot all contribute your ideas, so with
six people it is clear that you all can. Consequently if
one person does all the talking there is an implicit arrogance in his monopolizing the meeting. This points to
an important difference from larger presentations.

The difference is that with a larger audience you are
the speaker and they are the listeners, asking their questions when you invite them. But with a small group you
have to try and proceed by dialog instead of by monolog.
Even if the group shows a disposition to remain a silent,
passive audience, you must not let them. At every stage
you must invite them to participate: "Mr. Brown, you're
looking a bit worried—what have I got wrong?" "Mr.
Smith, you're closer to the practical side than I am—did
I leave something out?" "It's silly for me to invent examples—Mr. Jones, can you give me an instance of the
problems you're coming up against at the moment?" The
success of a presentation to a small group can be mea-
sured by the amount of time the presenter spends in
listening to and answering questions.

The disadvantage of a small group—that you are
spending your time getting through to only a handful
of people—is balanced by the fact that those few people
can be much more thoroughly convinced than a large
audience. They go away with their objections met, their

questions answered, and a sense of having thrashed the thing out. For this reason it tests the presenter's knowledge of his subject more searchingly. He must really know his ground and be very careful not to commit himself to assertions he cannot support from his own knowledge and experience.

Conversely, a small group puts less strain on presentation aids and techniques. Slides will hardly be necessary, since half a dozen people can look at a drawing or a photograph without optical enlargement. If slides are used, it will not matter if one or two come on upside down. The whole atmosphere is more relaxed, easy, and informal, and the presenter should keep it so. Nevertheless it is still a presentation, and all the principles stated earlier still apply. The presenter must plan what he has to say, and the order in which it has to be said. He must think himself into his audience's minds—though the dialog will be an enormous help to put him right where he goes wrong. He needs just as much care in selecting or designing the visuals he uses. He needs to vary the texture between words and pictures, between exposition and discussion. He needs to check that all aids and equipment are present and in working order. But the practicalities and the techniques need considerable modification.

The script. A formal prepared script, even in the most natural spoken English, is quite out of the question. The tone of the presentation is conversational dialog and must be spontaneous.

The shape. Spontaneous, however, does not mean unplanned. The presenter will have certain points to make in a certain order, and he must have these clearly in his head or written down in note form.

The texture. With such a small group it is not tolerable to hold the floor for more than a few minutes without letting members of the group have their turn. The exposition must therefore be broken down into small chunks with discussion time after each—and the exposition itself must be liberally punctuated with check-up questions like "Does that make sense?" Or "Are you still with me?"

Rehearsal. A formal rehearsal is by definition impossible. Nevertheless, a tryout with one or two colleagues as an audience is extremely valuable, especially if they can raise the sort of objections and questions you are likely to encounter.

Introduction. Notwithstanding the unscripted nature of these presentations, there are certain prerequisites for the introduction apart from the conventional welcoming courtesies. Always bear in mind:

1. Why they have come; that is, what you hope they will get out of the presentation.
2. Why you have asked them; that is, what you hope to show them or persuade them of.
3. The program; that is, the times of breaks and of visits to other buildings, and the practical arrangements like cars and train times.
4. The contents list; that is, the subjects you will be discussing and demonstrations you will be giving.

Visuals. These need to be simple and flexible. Of course any kind of visual aid can be used, but slides, overhead projectors, film, magnetic boards, and so on are unnecessarily complex, and if not handled in a very relaxed yet competent manner, can bring an unwelcome note of contrivance and formality. The best aids for this sort of presentation are:

Blackboard. It gives complete freedom to respond to any query that arises, and it can be handed over to any member of the audience who wants to make a visual point.

Pad and felt-tipped pen. Same as with the blackboard; and the additional advantage of not having to rub out and draw on traces of the last drawing. Best if mounted on an easel like a flip chart.

Drawings and still photographs. These are easy to show to a small group, making whatever points you want according to the degree and level of the audience's interest. You can also have a good supply of reserves which you do not plan to use but can produce if the conversation turns that way. A table lectern turned toward the group acts as a perfectly good stand if you want to leave one up for some time.

Solid objects. Anything you can pass around, or give people to keep, is much easier to do with a small group and just as effective.

Working models. Anything real that people can actually see working is even better with a small group than with a large one since everyone can have a go at operating it if it isn't too difficult or dangerous.

Portable film cassette projectors. These come into their own with small groups. They are often the only way of showing large equipment (airplanes, turbines, cranes, ships, machine tools) in operation.

But in general, this sort of presentation hinges on a blackboard or a pad and felt-tipped pen and drawings and still photographs. The more you give the impression that you had got it all planned in advance, the less convincing it will be.

It is dangerous to draw up rules about audiences, even to summarize a chapter; but the distinction seems to be that with large audiences you need maximum performing skill as a speaker, maximum slickness with visual aids and stage management, and a minimum number of questions; whereas with small audiences you need a maximum number of questions and answers, maximum informality, maximum flexibility of order and content, maximum knowledge of your subject, and minimum skill as a speaker and manipulator of visual aids. If you succeed with a large audience, they will be impressed and may change their attitudes. If you succeed with a small group they will be convinced and may change their minds.

8 / The Last Lap

By the time the day of the presentation arrives, almost all the factors that will determine its success or failure have been decided. If conception, planning, preparation, and rehearsal have been sensibly carried out and if proper thought has been given to words and pictures and the relationship between them, then 90 percent of the dangers have been removed. Presentations which look right at dress rehearsal very rarely go wrong, however inexperienced the presenters—despite the old theatrical superstition that a good dress rehearsal means a bad first night. Nevertheless there remain certain areas which still need attention, and where a bad slipup can be seriously disconcerting. You can never foresee everything, but most of the pitfalls can be avoided if you know where they are most likely to be.

Venue

The decision on where to hold the presentation will have been made early in the planning stage, and some of the considerations have nothing to do with the mechanics of the presentation itself. Is the location convenient for the audience to get to? Can we afford it? Is it posh enough? But if there is room for presentation factors to affect the choice, these are the main ones:

1. If you can possibly hold the presentation on your own premises, do so. It significantly reduces the area of the unforeseeable and uncontrollable.

2. If you have to choose between a room slightly too small and a room distinctly too large choose the smaller. Obviously if it is small to the point of discomfort, it is ruled out. But a lot of empty space is depressing. Churchill insisted that the rebuilt House of Commons should not have as many seats as there were MPs. It's much better to have them sitting in the aisles and standing at the back on the few great national occasions than to conduct most of the nation's business in a vast and almost empty cavern.

3. Should the audience sit in a few rows on a wide frontage or a lot of rows on a narrow frontage? I do not want to be dogmatic about this. I have a suspicion that an exact square may well be best. But failing that, I would use only the wide and shallow shape with a fairly small audience whom I wanted to treat extremely informally with a fair amount of questions and general conversation. If I wanted any sense of a show, or if the audience were over thirty, I would favor the narrow and deep alternative. There is an additional important consideration that also favors this, which is discussed later in this chapter under the heading "Stage Setting."

4. Avoid too large a gap between the presenter and the front row. The closer everyone is, the easier it is for him to hear and see, which is what presentation is all about.

5. An obvious element, but one which can be over-looked, is to check details of all technical facilities (lighting, projection, power supply, ventilation, fire regulations) far enough in advance to make any necessary changes.

6. Signpost corridors, if the building is at all labyrinthine, so that visitors can find their way to cloak rooms, buffets, bars, and the like—and back.

7. Sometimes the chosen venue is so booked up that a dress rehearsal on site cannot be arranged. If the presentation is at all important or complex this is a very grave liability, and serious thought should be given to holding it somewhere else. Dress rehearsal time should always be booked when the presentation time is itself being booked, usually for the previous day. The morning of an afternoon presentation is not as good—less time to get things done, and no chance to sleep on it all.

8. Have you got the room the wrong way round? Should the presentation area be at the other end? This matters if, for instance, interesting distractions will be going on outside a window behind the presenter in full view of the audience, or if the presenter is right next to the only door so that all messengers, accidental intruders, and late arrivals suddenly become part of the presentation as they open the door.

9. If you have not used the place for a presentation before, try and find someone who has and call him to find out if there are any snags or dodges to learn.

Dais Layout

For a lavish and expensive production you may want to employ a professional designer. Do not look on him as an esthetic mystic, and if he behaves like one get rid of him. Of course you expect him to have some sort of visual taste and color sense, but his chief talents are highly practical. He knows a large number of the visual opportunities and problems that arise, and he knows a wide range of techniques, materials, and devices for meeting them. It is for you to make sure that he knows what you are trying to do. The later you call him in, the less value he will be—you'll have already made a lot of his decisions yourself. The best time is suggested in Chapter 4, "Production Sessions." Don't tell him "We want an easel here, a green baize table here, and a blackboard here." Give him much more scope to help you. Tell him why you are doing the presentation, what you are hoping to achieve, and what the budget is, and ask him how he thinks you can best achieve what you want. The "why" is very important: A lectern encrusted with rhinestones may be an attractive idea, but not if the presentation is to tell a government department that you're so hard up that they must give you a research grant.

Lighting

There is a good deal of unnecessary mystique about lighting. Certainly some film and theater lighting can be extremely complex, but for presentations it is only a question of logic based on common sense. You are not likely to need to convey a slow sunrise, a thunderstorm, or a torchlight procession in the street below. Lighting for our purposes is simply to add clarity and focus attention, and logic says have lots of light on what you want the audience to look at and none anywhere else. Spot lighting is therefore usually better than general lighting, and it usually helps if it is fairly powerful. The speaker needs the strongest light (but not so as to cause him discomfort; put it high, not low into his eyeline), and all visual aids (charts, diagrams, blackboards, flip charts, models) need lighting projected from the place that causes least shadow when they are in use. It is attractive to fade up each visual aid spot as needed and fade it out afterward, but usually it is an unnecessary refinement. Stage spotlights have flaps called barn doors which you can close to stop light spilling where you don't want it. The chief place where you don't want it is the projection screen, if you have one. However, there is a story that an elderly lady member of a film society used to sit in the front row with a flashlight during foreign films, and shine it on the subtitles to help her to read them better.

Do not worry too much about lighting, however, for small presentations. General lighting will usually do well enough for audiences of up to forty or fifty people. Remember it can also help to focus attention on the whole presentation area. Sometimes the area can look rather lost in a large high room, but if the bulbs over it are replaced with the brightest possible ones and the flexes lengthened until the light is only about nine feet above the ground, it becomes far more of a focus of attention. (Also it casts an interesting shadow on the projection screen when slides are shown and shatters when you accidentally hit it with your pointer—but that's what dress rehearsals are for.)

If you want to try for lighting effects—fading up and down on appropriate places at appropriate points—remember that this requires a good knowledge of the script by the operator, and plenty of rehearsal. On the whole it is something to graduate to rather than start from.

Decor

Decor is not something to worry too much about. But sometimes the site has ugly pipes or unattractive walls, or distracting and irrelevant objects scattered around the place, and the judicious hanging of some reasonably colored curtains or some screening or cladding can help the general appearance and usefully enclose the presentation area. Remember that colored curtains often perk up wonderfully when you shine a bit of light on them. And get a woman to take a look at such things as the tables and chairs that you are using on the dais—masculine eyes sometimes fail to see unsightly jumbles of modern teak, Victorian mahogany, and reproduction Queen Anne in dark oak, which can easily be standardized if only someone thinks about it. After all, there may be some women in the audience, so you might as well have a similarly critical eye cast over things in advance.

The auditorium itself does not often need much in the way of decor. But don't forget, especially if you're going to have coffee and tea breaks, that attractive and informative display panels around the room can give people something to look at and also supply factual details that you do not want to weigh the presentation down with. If you are having breaks or a buffet lunch in a different room, you can have your display panels there.

Stage Setting

The problem of stage setting begins only when you have a number of objects on the stage, and especially if there is a slide projection screen at the back. Then it can be quite a headache. The specific problem is sight lines. You always find that, from one side of the audience or the other, something is obstructing the view of something else. Usually an easel or flip chart is in front of the projection screen. Every time you move it you get another problem—different obstruction, light spill, masking by presenter, or something else. There's no general solution, it's just a three-dimensional jigsaw puzzle that you have to solve as best you can—but you must realize in time that you are setting it for yourself. The only general principle (as referred to earlier in this chapter) is that the narrower the audience frontage, the easier the problem is to solve. With a really wide frontage it can border on the impossible.

On the more positive side, it always helps if the stage has an appetizing look for the audience when they arrive. Not just in the orthodox design sense, but it should have the look of a place where interesting things are about to happen. So don't always conceal all the things you don't want immediately; leave them out—or leave them on the stage in an attractive box.

Stage Management

By stage management I don't just mean operations on the day of the presentation; stage management is an aspect of the planning of the whole presentation, and it involves visualizing the whole sequence.

Thinking through the sequence. Think the whole thing through in your mind pictorially and in detail—especially the junction points. Work out exactly what will happen and what objects and actions will be needed at every point. How does x get off the dais? Where does he go? How does y get on? Where does he come from? Do they hand over the microphone or leave it on the lectern? Who has the pointer? Are the flip charts on from the start or do we set them up after the presentation begins? How does the projectionist know when to run the film? There are hundreds of questions like these to be sorted out, resulting in a number of checks to be made before the presentation starts and certain actions to be taken while it is in progress. A checklist and notes in the script margin are the only answers, and if it is a big presentation, this needs to be one man's responsibility, though he may well be one of the understudies.

What if . . . ? After all the questions based on the assumption that things go right, there is another sequence which start "What if . . . ?" based on the most possible of the most critical failures. What if the projector breaks down? What if the microphone doesn't work? What if the model doesn't arrive from the factory? Once the question is asked, the action to be taken is usually fairly clear, but it may involve preparations, so it must be asked in time. Experienced stage managers usually have certain standard equipment always in their pocket: chalk, felt pen, drawing pins, sticky tape, penknife, razor blade, string, wire, and nail file seem to be the most frequently employed—the nail file is used as screwdriver and thin steel lever, and not for cosmetic purposes.

Microphones. If you cannot get by with the unaided human voice, sound coverage is rarely completely satisfactory. A microphone on the table is all right until the speaker goes to the blackboard, then it loses him. If he takes it with him it is a nuisance and volume varies depending on where he holds it. A lanyard microphone, hung round the neck like a pendant, solves that problem, but you still have to worry about tripping over the cable or bringing the easel down with it. And it can be awkward to hand over if there is more than one presenter—it looks as if each speaker is investing his successor with the Man of the Year award. To overcome the cable problem you can use a radio microphone which has no cable, just a small high-frequency transmitter. I used this once for a presentation to 2000 people in Leeds City Hall, and it turned out to be operating on the same frequency as the Leeds radiocab service. Taxidrivers' conversations blared across the hall at beautifully chosen points throughout the presentation. You can't win. Even if it is working perfectly, the speakers usually mistrust it and scratch it with their fingernails and say "Can you hear me?—testing—one-two-three . . ." in jargon they have picked up from the post-office mechanics. Do without microphones if you can, and get plenty of rehearsal in with them if you can't.

External interruptions. Some noises are outside your building and your control. You will never foresee all the possible ones, but it helps if you are alert for them. Is the building on an air traffic route because of certain wind conditions? Even your first visit may not tell you that, depending on wind direction. Are pneumatic drills going to be operating in the street? Does the children's playground outside the window make presentation impossible during their break and lunch hour? Here too you may learn less painfully from other people's experience than from your own.

Internal interruptions. As with external interruptions you can draw on other people's experience, but it is easier to be there on the day of the week and at the time of day your presentation is planned for and see if any snags crop up. Does a noisy potato peeling machine start up in the kitchens above the presentation room at 11:30 A.M.?

Is there a fire alarm and practice just on the day of your presentation? Do canteen workers play table tennis next door between 3 and 4:30 P.M.? When does the window cleaner get around to this room? Do cups and glasses clatter past to the directors' dining room from 12 to 12:30? Are people going to barge in thinking the room is empty if you don't put a sign on the door? Will four men be taking the carpet away for cleaning as the audience arrives? Again, you can never anticipate every possible interruption: The readiness is all.

Dress Rehearsal

Try and take the dress rehearsal right through without any interruptions. If you pause you sometimes miss snags which continuity would have revealed. Make notes and go through them carefully at the end. It is sometimes a good idea to invite someone, who up till now has had nothing to do with the presentation, to look at it with a fresh eye. But this is no time to start criticizing the presenters. There are two purposes in the dress rehearsal:

1. To try out an already well-rehearsed presentation in its actual location and see if any unexpected problems crop up because of the place and its circumstances and facilities.
2. To give those involved in the presentation experience and encouragement.

To have done the presentation in the actual territory is a source of confidence, and at this stage people want all the confidence they can get. It is a time for praise and congratulations and encouragement, and any visitors should know this in advance. Serious worries should be voiced in private to the man in charge. If correction has to be made at this stage it must be phrased most tactfully ("I wonder whether it wouldn't be even more effective if . . .") and followed up with unstinted praise ("That slide sequence goes marvellously now."). Professional actors sometimes need to have the fear of God put into them at this stage. With presenters I have found it is usually already there in abundance—it is hope of salvation they are short of.

The Presentation

Oddly enough, there isn't very much to say about the presentation itself. Or perhaps it isn't so odd; it is what the whole book has been about. The only special factor is first-night nerves, a kind of tension that communicates itself to everyone and can impair performance and make people lose their heads and do stupid things. Most people have some sort of butterflies-in-the-tummy feeling before doing a piece in public, and this is quite normal and natural. It is when the butterflies get out into the atmosphere that the trouble begins.

If there is any danger of this, the temperature must be deliberately lowered at the run-through stage by the producer of the presentation. He must adopt a deliberately casual approach, no sentences must start "Whatever happens, for God's sake don't . . ." He must appear to be taking the smoothness of the final presentation for granted. At the presentation itself, there must be no urgent whispered colloquy followed by someone hastening off at a thinly disguised run.

It also helps a lot if those who will be doing the presenting have a chance to meet their audience informally before they start. A brief chat over a cup of coffee together can thaw out the atmosphere wonderfully. The presenters may even realize that their audience do presentations themselves from time to time, and feel much the same about it. Then, if the most easy, natural, and relaxed of the presenters does his piece first, you can begin to create the atmosphere you want—though the larger the audience the harder it is.

And in the right atmosphere, nothing can go really wrong. Even a disaster can be a plus. The damaging thing when the blackboard falls over is the presenter's shame, not the small interruption to the flow of his talk. If he sees the joke, shares it, and caps it, it can win over the audience to his side wonderfully. I once saw a presenter give a demonstration that showed how a computer worked by sending tennis balls through a series of gates into a register selected by a program which was another set of tennis balls. He explained how they would all go into register seven, forgot to load the program, released them, and they shot straight into the zero. The audience rocked with laughter. He clutched his head in delighted, theatrical distress, enjoying it with them. When the laughter subsided he said "That's exactly what I was saying. The computer is plain stupid. It does whatever you tell it, however crazy. A child of five would have heard what I was saying and put the data into the seven register. But the computer is a zombie—never helps you out. But if you program it *correctly*, it never lets you down." It was much better than getting it right the first time, and in fact he kept the mistake in forever afterwards. It is not the disaster which is the disaster—it is the presenter's wrong reaction to it.

And suppose you can tell that the whole presentation is going badly—that there are impatient snuffles and shuffles coming out of the audience? It is difficult to cut and rearrange a complex presentation as it's running, but it may be possible. Speakers may speed up a bit, but there's not a lot they can do. Sometimes it's a good idea to have a question session at the next junction, or even to ask them if there are things they are more interested in than what the program contains, and dissolve the presentation into a seminar. After all, it is the audience you are doing it for. If they dislike it, there is not much point in gritting your teeth and going right on and the hell with them.

Afterwards

So it's all over. It was a great success, everyone did splendidly, and a mood of euphoria settles on everyone. This is no time for cool appraisals but warm congratulations. ("Oh, do you really think it went all right?" which is English for "Don't stop praising me, I'm enjoying it.") But if it was really a success, the chances are that you will be called on to give other presentations and that this one will have generated a lot of raw experience which can be worked into a body of knowledge. A week or more later is the time to talk over the lessons that were learned, if possible with all those who played an important part in the presentation and with someone who was in the audience for the first time and who took notes. This is the only real way to learn about visual presentation. A book is like a map—it gives a picture of the terrain, it shows the good and bad routes, the culs-de-sac and shortcuts, the dangerous cliffs and the quagmires. But it does not actually get you anywhere—you still have to make the journey yourself. I hear and forget; I see and remember; I do and understand.

9 / Commissioning a Film

A_{ny} important presentation is liable to need a film sequence or sequences specially shot; furthermore, a film is itself a presentation of a particularly durable, controllable, and usually expensive kind. Film making is of course a task for specialists and beyond the scope of this book, but anyone concerned with presentations may at some time have to commission a film, and unless it is done right (and it is easy to do wrong) it is a very quick way of wasting a lot of time, effort, and money. Also someone who needs a film may be deterred by simply not knowing how to set about it. So here are some basic guidelines which, while they cannot insure a good film, will enable anyone who follows them to avoid nearly all the obstacles that stop good films from happening.

Do You Really Want a Film?

It is easy to say "We need a film," and the idea is an intoxicating one. The very word "film" awakens echoes of Cecil B. de Mille and Elizabeth Taylor and swimming pools in Beverly Hills. But perhaps your purposes would be better served by a book, a live presentation sequence, or a sequence of stills printed onto film with an added commentary so that you show it through a projector but never employ a movie camera. Film has several disadvantages.

1. It is expensive, often unnecessarily so since the details are usually outside the comprehension of the sponsor.

2. It is a pig in a poke—you can't see it before you buy it, and when you can see it it's too late to discover it's not what you wanted.

3. It prohibits participation—you can't ask a film a question.

4. It is inflexible—you can't adapt it for special audiences as you can adapt a live presentation.

5. It can be outdated—new buildings, equipment, products, policies, names, and faces can make it obsolete before full value has been extracted from it.

6. It takes a longish time from conception to execution and can be at the mercy of second, third, and fourth thoughts.

7. Chairmen, presidents, chief executives, and board members who would never dream of dropping in on a presentation will often order a screening of a film. Fear of this can create jitters among subordinates resulting in the removal of anything arresting or original from the film.

The advantages are more obvious: It is the most complete and powerful form of communication, it commands total attention in a way the printed word cannot; it can bring before people's eyes pictures of things that move, collected from all over the world, through telescopes and microscopes and stroboscopes, in fast or slow motion; you can constantly adjust pictures and words until you have them right. Then you can distribute prints all over the world knowing that it will be shown in the form you intended. Inflexibility is also reliability. Nevertheless, it is a mistake to assume that there is a need for a film before properly analyzing the objectives and alternative means of achieving them.

Who Should Make the Film?

The film is going to succeed or fail because of two men: One is you, the sponsor, and the other is the film maker. How do you find one?

Look at some films. It is a great risk to get a film made by someone whose films you have not seen. If you have seen a film that you thought good, and it was also the kind of film you want, approach the maker of it. But the kind of film is important: A good film of engineering processes is no guide to someone's ability in putting over theoretical concepts. If someone is recommended, look at one or two of his films before you meet him.

Films are made by people, not companies. You are looking for the man who made the film you liked, not the company. Of course he may still be with the company, but in this sort of business people move around quite a lot. Be very cautious about putting yourself in the hands of a film company unless you have seen a range of good films by it which a variety of different people have written and directed.

Who makes a film? How do you know who the man was who actually made the film? Is he called producer or director? There is no answer to the second question. The answer to the first can be obtained by a call to the people the film was made for. They are always clear about who was answerable to them for the success or failure of the film, and whether he was called producer or director or production supervisor doesn't matter a damn.

What should you look for in a film? This is almost impossible to answer without descending into laborious detail or retreating into mystical words like "flair" and "impact" which are almost meaningless. The best guide is a purely personal one—your feeling about the film as it ends; if it leaves you with the feelings and attitudes which it set out to arouse, it has succeeded. It set out to make you believe that half the accidents in engineering shops could be avoided by a single half-hour induction course for all recruits, and you left the film convinced that this was so; fine, that is the main point of it all. Second, you never got bored; the film always kept you wanting to know what was coming next. Third, you could take it all in; nothing was too padded or too compressed or too confusing, either visually or verbally, and there were no stretches of commentary too long to listen to. Fourth, it was properly thought out; it had the right facts and the right pictures in the right places to make its points. Fifth, it was all relevant; there were no sequences which added nothing and could have been left out. If those five conditions are met, you are on to a good thing. Dramatic climax, sidesplitting humor, breathtaking pictures, unbearable suspense—all these are splendid if you can employ them and afford them, but I'd settle for the more mundane standards of efficiency.

What should you look for in a producer? This question is almost more difficult to answer than, What should you look for in a film? Certainly the producer should have an open mind about what sort of film it should be, until he has a good understanding of what you want to achieve. It is a danger sign if he seems more concerned with the picture he is going to make than with the objectives you want to achieve. It's also a danger sign if he doesn't ask many questions or admit his own ignorance about your subject and if he gives the impression that he can achieve whatever you want. He ought to be referring your aspirations to the realities of budget and cameras and microphones and audiences. It's another danger sign if he seems concerned only with satisfying you, rather than with satisfying the audience you want to show the film to. And, although in principle I dislike this kind of advice, it is important that you should feel you can get on with him. The sponsor-producer relationship can be subjected to quite severe pressures, and even the smallest hint of mistrust, suspicion, or incompatibility can be fatal to the film.

If you cannot find anyone you really feel in your heart you want to make this film with, you should really think very seriously about whether to go on with it. Much better abandon it now than go ahead with the best of a bad bunch.

The Sponsor and the Producer

All right, you've chosen your man—let's call him the producer. His films have impressed you; the other sponsors speak well of him. He's interested, he asks intelligent questions, he seems to understand something of your sort of business, you trust him, and you like him. You are already halfway home, and it doesn't matter if it took a great deal of time and trouble to find him. The choice of the producer is by far the most significant single determinant of the success of the film. However, you and he are different kinds of animal, and a chasm still divides you. You must set about building a bridge.

The chasm is a communication chasm. You understand your firm's business backward—its history, its power structure, its internal tensions, its external successes and failures, its pride, and its prejudices. He knows virtually nothing of this. He does know, however, about bench-work and stop-frame animation and cranes and dollies and synch pulse tape, and when he talks about hand-held Eclairs it never occurs to him that you think he means something you eat at a tea party. He commands a wide range of tools and techniques for achieving your objectives—but he does not yet know what your objectives are, and he will not understand if you tell him since he does not yet have the background knowledge to give him a frame of reference.

This brings us to the crux of the relationship, and many films founder because it is not properly understood. Think for a moment in terms of an architect designing a house for you. You do not draw him the house you want—if you're that expert, all you need is a building contractor. You tell him how much you can afford and how you want to use the house and the priorities. It's his job to offer you suggestions and alternatives. Is a south aspect more important than a large back garden? Do you want to eat in the kitchen? Is good sound insulation more important than good heat insulation? Had you thought of laminating the kitchen window sills? Do you realize that by moving these two radiators nearer the center of the house you could manage with a smaller boiler? He is constantly forcing you to think harder about what you really want and getting more and more insight into your objectives.

In this respect a film producer is very like an architect. If you tell him the pictures you want and the commentary you want, you are usurping his role and wasting his talents. He can almost certainly do better for you than that. To bridge the chasm, you must help him to the fullest possible understanding of the end result you are trying to achieve, and he must offer you suggestions and alternatives. He will begin to see what you are after; you will begin to see the implications of various decisions. If the film is to be highly technical, it cannot also be shown to schools for recruitment. If you want to film in the African factory you cannot also afford the cartoon sequence. If you have lots of people talking on camera, there will be problems in the foreign language versions. And so on. This is quite a long dialog, and you must not try to rush it. You should also encourage the producer to talk to other members of the firm, if only to sort out what is generally accepted and what is just your point of view.

The producer's authority. One other point must be established from the start, and that is the producer's authority. It must be made clear to him, and more particularly to all your subordinates, that he takes orders from you and you alone. There is a special reason why this is important: Everybody who holds any authority under you is likely to feel responsible for what is in the film if they are involved in it or are asked questions. And they are also likely to dread that the moment the chairman sees the film they will be fired. This induces a paralyzing caution, a determination to agree to nothing except the most innocuous and trite words and pictures. If they know it is not their responsibility, the terror is removed.

This of course is all very well if you are making the film on your own authority, from your own budget, and for your own purpose. If your boss is doing this but has delegated it to you, make him read this chapter and think again. There remains the possibility that you are responsible to a committee. This can work perfectly well provided certain conditions are met:

1. The committee must be small—not more than three or four people, plus you and the producer—and representative. You don't want the most pliable or the most progressive, you want sensible middle-of-the-road people.

2. The committee must be taken fully into the producer's confidence and really talk things through at the earliest stages, before shooting. This not only helps the producer, it also implicates the committee in the film if they have agreed to the salient points.

3. The committee must give full editorial authority to the producer. They retain, of course, the right to be consulted, the right of veto on grounds of fact or policy, and the right to scrap the whole thing. But if they have editorial authority they are answerable to their colleagues for everything that is included, everything that is omitted, and the way everything is done. So heavy a burden may break their nerve. Much easier if they can say "Yes, we didn't like that bit either, but we had the power only to advise or veto; we couldn't improve anything." A wise producer will ask for that editorial freedom before he goes ahead, and he has no reason or incentive to abuse it.

Agreeing on objectives. The purpose of the dialog between the sponsor (with or without the advisory committee) and the producer is to reach agreement on an objective which both of them fully understand. A useful means to this end is to define your key audience—a new graduate thinking about a career, the production manager of an engineering firm, the chief executive of a medium-sized company—and then to formulate the sentence you want to be in the audience's mind when the projector stops and the lights go up. This agreement about objectives demands great honesty from the sponsor. The producer must be told about departmental rivalries and jealousies which will make certain desirable ingredients difficult and dangerous; he must be told where the firm has unsuccessful products or a bad reputation; and he must be told of subsidiary, even if ignoble, motives behind the commissioning of the film. ("Marketing did a good film last year which made quite a star out of the marketing director, and the production director really agreed to this out of personal jealousy, so it will be difficult to leave him out completely.")

Part of the difficulty in getting the dialog under way is that dialog is conducted with words, but films are made with pictures. Inevitably when you decided on a film you had certain pictures in mind, and you may believe you have conveyed them to the producer: You probably haven't. So do not be ashamed to draw lots of very bad rough sketches in screen-shaped boxes to show him what you mean, but make it clear that your purpose is not to make him take those pictures, only to convey to him what you are thinking of.

Practical Decisions

Before the film gets under way, you will be asked to make certain practical decisions, all of them important and some of them irreversible. It is well to be aware of their implications.

What gauge? In practice this means "Do you want the film shot in 35 millimeter or 16 millimeter?" Almost all industrial films are shot on 16 millimeter for three very good reasons:

1. It is significantly cheaper.
2. The camera is more portable so shooting is easier, quicker, and therefore often more enterprising.
3. The film is almost always going to be shown by people with 16 mm, not 35 mm, projectors.

You would think of 35 mm only if you had need for extra special picture quality or if the film was likely to be shown in full-size cinemas where the screen enlargement is so great that 16 mm looks messy. A film shot on 35 mm can always be reduced to 16 mm.

Color or black and white? Most people shoot in color nowadays, and other things being equal it is almost always preferable. But other things can be very unequal, because the costs are quite a lot higher. This starts to matter if the shooting ratio is likely to be high. The shooting ratio is the ratio of film exposed to film used. If 2½ hours of film are exposed and the film runs 30 minutes, the ratio is 5:1—which incidentally is fairly economical. If you are making a film with sequences where the camera has to run for a long time in the hope of some brief incident, the ratio can go up to 20:1 or higher. In that case the cost differential between color and black and white becomes much larger, and it is worth finding out how much you could save and discussing whether there are ways of spending the money that would give better value.

How long should the film run? If you run the film longer than 25 or 30 minutes, you are setting yourself a lot of problems. The chief one is holding the audience's attention—the film needs to be quite a lot better as entertainment if it goes over half an hour. It is also harder to get people to give up the best part of an hour of their time rather than just 20 minutes or so, and if the film is ever to be used in discussions or seminars a shorter film gives time for introduction and discussion within a 40-minute period.

Setting About It

Before you commit yourself to a film maker you should establish two stages at which you can pull out— after the treatment and after the shooting script.

The treatment. All too often the treatment is just a sales document disguised as an outline of the film: "The film will show in compelling and vivid detail . . . dramatically contrasting . . . leading the audience into the throbbing heart of . . . rising to a climax . . ." and so on. All you are looking for is a simple outline of what will be shown and said in the film, and you will judge from that whether the producer understands what you are trying to achieve. It should not be more than a page or two long, but it may cost four or five hundred dollars, since if it is to be done properly there is a fair amount of preliminary research and discussion to be carried out first. My own view is that a good treatment is so much more important than anything else that it is often worth paying double what it might ordinarily cost so that the producer can afford to spend a longer time getting to understand your objectives before committing himself to paper. Once he has decided on a treatment, it is hard for him to put it all back in the melting pot.

The shooting script. Unlike the treatment, the shooting script is an operational document. It is usually divided into two columns, one saying what the audience will see, shot by shot, and the other saying what they will hear. It is the nearest you will get to seeing the film you are commissioning before you commit yourself to pay for it. But it is all too easy for a layman to misunderstand it. To start with, it is almost impossible to see how music, sound effects, camera work, and editing will combine to produce an effect on the audience. In addition, the picture column is full of jargon—mix, track, pan, dissolve, m.c.u. (medium close-up), w/a (wide angle), s/i (superimpose), and the rest of it—which diverts concentration from the commentary/dialog column. This however is most misleading when just read on its own, and in the case of commentary can be changed even after the filming is over. The shooting script only commits you to pictures and synchronous sound. So do not hope to judge from the shooting script whether it will be a good film. Look for errors of fact, pictures wrongly included or whose significance seems to be misunderstood, and pictures omitted which you think should be included.

When reading and discussing the shooting script—and this applies at all later stages as well—there is one vital point to bear in mind. The producer, if he is any good, is not making this film to show to you or your company; he is making it for the audiences you are going to show it to. A paean of unqualified praise lasting 30 minutes may delight all the members of the company, but it will leave everyone else cold. He, as an outsider, is likely to be a better judge than you of how to interest the audience. The company may judge the film by whether it says and shows all the things they want said and shown, but its success (assuming it is not being made exclusively for internal use) will depend on how many people outside the company see it. The more interesting and enjoyable it is for them, the more attention they will pay to it and the more they will recommend it—and also the more respect they will have for people capable of holding their interest.

It is hard to say how much you should pay for a shooting script—it may involve a lot of time by the producer, director, and writer, even including overseas travel. It is probably best to agree to a rejection fee before you commission it—a sum to be paid if you decide not to go ahead after completion of the shooting script. You must expect it to be three or four times as much as the cost of the treatment. If you do go ahead, it becomes part of the total cost of the film.

Budget

Once the shooting script is complete, it is possible to make up a reasonably accurate budget. Some film companies may try and present it to you as a single, global figure, but you should make it clear from the start that you will want a detailed breakdown before going ahead. This is not so much because it is harder to fiddle a detailed budget as to give you an opportunity to understand the cost implications of various production decisions. You may have asked for shots in factories in five different cities: The travel and subsistence figure will prompt an inquiry into how much cheaper it would be to take them all in one city. The special equipment bill may reveal to you that a casual remark of yours about taking a wide shot of the milling shop when it's empty has been translated into a vast lorry load of lights being driven down from London, with weekend overtime rates for everyone. An example of the sort of budget breakdown you will need is included at the end of this chapter, but generally speaking the expensive variables which can be reduced by modifying the shooting script are

1. Animation, especially cartoon animation.
2. The lighting of large areas for a single shot (expensive not only for the extra lights but also for the time it takes setting up).
3. Using a full sound crew when a silent camera would do almost as well.
4. Travel, especially overseas, and subsistence. Quite apart from the direct expense, crew time is spent traveling instead of filming. Think about including still photographs of remote locations you would like to include, or—for overseas filming—getting a local cameraman to take some shots and send them back to you.
5. Night and weekend shooting when overtime has to be paid.
6. Outside location shooting when special weather conditions are essential; for example, where you may have to spend days just waiting for bright sunlight, heavy rain, or snow. If almost any weather conditions will do, outside location filming—since normally it needs no lights—is quick and cheap.

There is one other important budget consideration, and that is the payment of the producer. If the film is being made by a film company which has its own cameras and editing machines, their profit will be a percentage of the total cost. This of course gives them an incentive to make the film as expensive as possible. If this worries you, it may be possible to engage an independent producer and agree to his fee irrespective of the budget.

He will then have an incentive to work with you to keep all the other costs as low as possible.

It must also be understood that once the budget is agreed to, it is not just a general guide for you; it is a firm undertaking by the producer or the film company that the film will be delivered for that sum.

The Point of No Return

Once you have agreed to the shooting script and the budget and have given the go-ahead, you have passed the point of no return. There is very little you can do to affect the film until shooting is completed. It is usually wise, however, to fix the following dates by agreement with the producer and check periodically that they are not slipping—or not too badly: (a) The date filming will start. (b) The date filming will end. (c) The date you will be able to see a rough cut. The rough cut is the next point at which you get involved in the film. It is a rough assembly of the pictures in sequence, but probably a good 50 percent longer than the final version, and it is not likely to have any commentary. As with the shooting script, it is hard for a layman to foresee or deduce the final effect of the completed film by seeing the rough cut. At this stage the producer and his team need confidence and encouragement, and unless you are gravely worried you should try and give them some. If you can see that it is all hopeless, that nothing you wanted is there, you can cut your losses by calling the whole thing off straightaway, but you will probably not be able to save more than 20 percent of the budget from the wreck. But if the rough cut includes most of the pictures you wanted, you will serve your own purposes best by distributing general praise and admiration. You can then get down to details, and the details that concern you are not those that make it a good or bad film: They are those on which you are specially qualified to speak—factual and pictorial accuracy, order of sequences, company policy, and the intention and objectives of the film as a whole. Be particularly careful to mention what you think is important to keep in, because there is still quite a lot of cutting to do. After you've seen the rough cut, fix a date for seeing the final assembly with commentary.

You may be sent a copy of the commentary to read, though experience has made many producers reluctant to do this. If you do receive a copy, for heaven's sake don't start rewriting it; it is intimately related to pictures, music, and sound effects in ways you cannot possibly know about. Make your comments on a separate sheet of paper, and try to restrict them to what is wrong with the commentary rather than what you recommend as possible alterations: "This does not give the most important fact . . ." "This emphasizes the wrong aspect . . ." "This gives the impression that we only . . ." "This figure is the national, not the world production . . ." Treat it as you would a fitting at the tailor's: You tell him where the suit feels too tight or too loose or hangs badly, but you would never dream of getting out a piece of chalk and drawing marks on the cloth. A commentary is tailor-made to the film in the same way, and you have no business carrying out the alterations yourself.

The trouble with commentary is that it looks so easy to alter, and consequently a great many films are killed by commentary which might otherwise have survived and flourished. The lethal element in commentary is the overdose. A good film will leave many gaps in commentary, and the story will be taken forward by pictures with sound effects or music or actuality sound. Commentary alterations usually mean additions, and the vital gaps start to disappear, with the self-defeating result that the audience simply cannot take any of it in. In particular try to restrain yourself from asking for additional words for company rather than audience reasons: "The Birmingham factory will be unhappy if we don't mention . . ." "The research people would like it if we said that they . . ." and so on. There is a limit to what the audience can absorb as film commentary, and the writer is trying to keep it simple and sparing. Of course you must correct errors of fact, emphasis, omission, and policy, but you would do well to think of the overall duration of each paragraph as immutable.

Once the commentary is agreed upon, the film is complete as far as you are concerned. There is nothing to do but fix a date for the delivery of the final print, invite the guests to the premier, and make sure the drinks are served before the viewing—and liberally.

Note: SPECIMEN FILM BUDGET BREAKDOWN

Total

Studio, crew, and equipment time
_____ days studio hire @ $_____ per day   _____
_____ days silent filming @ $_____ per day   _____
_____ days sound filming @ $_____ per day   _____
_____ days editing and negative cutting
    @ $_____ per day   _____
_____ days dubbing @ $_____ per day   _____
_____ days extra equipment hire @ $_____
    per day   _____
_____ days extra lighting hire @ $_____ per
    day   _____

Total

Film stock and processing
———— feet exposed negative @ $——— per foot ————
———— feet rushes print @ $——— per foot ————
———— feet reprints @ $——— per foot
———— feet sound stock @ $——— per foot ————
———— feet final print @ $——— per foot ————

Travel and subsistence
———— days car mileage @ $——— per day ————
———— days extra car hire @ $——— per day ————
———— days subsistence @ $——— per day ————
Train fares (details) ———————————— ————
Boat fares (details) ———————————— ————
Air fares (details) ———————————— ————
Freight charges (details) ———————————— ————
Entertainment, permissions, facilities ————

Special film effects
Titles and graphic work ————
Animation ————
Benchwork ————
Still photography ————
Optical effects ————

Artists, rights, and the like
Music rights ————
Copyright ————
Stills copyright ————
Film copyright (library film) ————
Actors or narrators or both ————
Musicians ————

Production
Scenery, props, makeup ————
Producer ————
Director ————
Writer ————
Designer ————
Administration and overhead ————
  Add 10 percent contingency ————
    Total ————

10 / Writing Film
Commentary

Just occasionally you may have to write the commentary to a piece of film yourself—for instance, when the film is suitable pictorially, but has the wrong words. It is a specialist's craft but not impossible for a good presenter to have a go at, provided he starts on something not too difficult.

Film commentary is still a form of writing for speech, so the guidelines in Chapter 5 still need to be followed. But it is also the most complete form of audio-visual communication, since the whole time you are writing you must be conscious of what the audience are seeing, what they have already seen, and what they are about to see. At every stage it is the *combined* impact you must consider. The implications of this are considerable.

Practicalities

Even the practicalities are complicated. Once the film has started running, it goes on running at precisely the same speed until it's finished. Its pace cannot be varied at all. No one, in other words, can hurry the film up if it's behind the commentary or slow it down if it's ahead. It is a constant. Therefore it's the writer who must make sure that what he has written fits the film at every point. For this reason it is extremely risky to give any but the briefest or most general commentary "live" during the presentation. A coughing spasm, a dropped page of notes, any interruption, and you are out of touch with your picture or you leave out something that was important to say. ("The cooling towers . . . No, sorry, that's the chairman and managing director. It was the cooling towers we saw before. I meant to say they were incredibly thick—the cooling towers I mean, not the chairman and, oh sorry, this is the rolling mill . . .") If you are not to risk this sort of fiasco, you must record your commentary in advance.

If you look at a roll of film and a roll of commentary recorded on magnetic tape, you will see, if you visualize them running, how words exist in time rather than space—this word is five seconds in, this one six seconds, and so on, and they are parallel to the changing picture. But how do you know that what you write will correspond to the pictures on the screen? Well, you know that a normal speaker speaks three words a second, or two words to each foot of 35 mm film. So you can always count back and know at what point in time your sentence or paragraph starts and ends, and the time at any point in it. You also have a shot list, which is a description of the shot in the left-hand column, and cumulative duration on the right. So it will tell you for example that there's a shot of a house (5 seconds), a man comes out the door (5 to 10 seconds), walks down road (10 to 20 seconds), goes into a police station (20 to 27 seconds), door shuts at 27, and so on. And by counting the words you have written and referring to the shot list, you should be able to see what word plus what picture the viewer is hearing and seeing at any given second of the film.

Writer and Film Editor

So much for the bare mechanics. They're the least interesting part of the business. What about the conventions—who is the film commentator? This matters because it affects how you write in all sorts of ways. And I think the best way to think of yourself is as the chap who has already seen the film and is sitting beside the audience watching it with them, and making it more enjoyable for them by what you say. Explaining, elucidating, adding interest to the pictures, explaining their importance, directing their eyes sometimes to certain parts of the screen, sometimes to others, re-creating the atmosphere, building suspense, and above all shutting up when they just want to look. You shouldn't deceive them by pretending you do not know what is coming next or, by using a phony present tense, pretending it is happening now. What you say and what they are seeing are always so complementary that they cannot tell if your words have been written to fit the pictures, or the pictures have been shot and edited to fit your words.

But, and this is a vital point, it will virtually always be the former. The writer starts when the film editor stops. The writer must accept the discipline of the film editor— at least until he understands about film editing. What I mean is that the writer cannot play merry hell with the film, make the editor change the order, lengthen sequences, and so on, because of what he wants to write. The editor has a story to tell too. He arranges the pictures so that they have a visual logic, a flow which tells the story as far as the pictures can. You may want to say

"Outside the workshop there are finished parts; inside, parts are being machined. Outside are packaging teams and dispatch clerks, inside are setters and operators. Outside, the revving of lorry engines, inside the screech of machine tools." It may read all right, but it's visual chaos. The picture has to dart inside and out all the time, the viewer is confused, and the visual flow of the story is shattered. You might try it once a year for a special effect, but it probably would not work even then. In film terms it is nearly always better to get that sort of effect with a full sequence inside and then a full sequence outside, so the eye has a good chance to take in and assimilate one visual idea at a time.

The same applies to shot lengths. The editor may decide that a static long shot of the Eiffel Tower is worth three seconds. You may have a beautiful 100-word story about the Eiffel Tower. You cannot make him continue the shot another thirty seconds to let you tell it. Once the eye has fully assimilated the Eiffel Tower, it is bored, and you might as well tell your story over a blank screen, because once the picture has died the screen is virtually blank anyway. Or tell it when the film is over. This is not to say that there can be no give and take between writer and editor—of course there is a lot. But it is always on the basis of pooling their skills to produce a better combined word-and-picture effect, not the editor making the film worse to help the writer out of a spot. In fact, as you improve as a commentary writer, you can't help becoming something of an editor and something of a director.

Words and Pictures

So we have established our convention and the relationship of the writer and editor. Now let us look at the relationship between word and picture. Here the writer has tremendous scope, despite the restrictions imposed by the discipline. There is a popular assumption that any single piece of film says only one thing. The writer's scope lies in the fact that many single pieces of film are capable of saying all sorts of things, depending on the writer's wish. However it does lead to an important point: The less the content of your commentary is connected to the film, the more connected it must appear to be. You do not say "people" but "people like these" to stop the viewer from wondering whether you are talking about the same picture that he is watching. You do not say "in London" but "here in London." Some words are drawing pins for fixing the commentary to the film— "this" and "these," "here," "like this"—you need them all the time. If what you are saying is really rather general, then you have to make a special effort to drag the picture into it somehow. As just stated, the less the commentary actually refers to the picture, the more it must seem to. In particular, try and refer to it at the very start of the sentence. If the first shot is of a lot of English people, once you have started "These people will have to decide . . ." you can go on about almost anything. Conversely, if you start with "The Italians can never understand . . . ," the force of association would have made it appear you were saying the people in the picture were Italians, even if the whole sentence was "The Italians can never understand why the English look so miserable."

Logical Flow

So the commentary must fit the picture, even if it is largely syntactic sleight of hand. And of course there must always be some real relationship as well. What else? It must also have a flow of its own. I have talked about the film that looks chaotic if the commentary is taken away—the film simply cut to fit words and not for its own visual logic. There is also the commentary that sounds absurd without the film—just a chain of unconnected remarks referring to a succession of changing pictures. As the film has a visual logic and flow of visual sequences, so the commentary must have a logical flow as well; it must have a spine and a shape. A narrative film usually has the basic flow of chronology though the good storyteller often adds something else—a question that is not answered until the end of the film; for instance, Will the ship be built on time by the new method? Will the engine perform in practice the way it did in the bench test? But at least the chronology is there anyway. With film that is not narrative it is often even more necessary to have a theme you can start on, refer to, and end with, to complement the roundedness of the pictures.

Another enemy of flow is the temptation to write film commentary as if you were captioning still photographs. It rarely works, and single sentences barked out at intervals with pauses fail more often than they succeed. I don't know why this should be. The single short sentence is sometimes highly effective; but as a *way* of commentary writing it gets very tedious. Somehow the paragraph seems to work better, even if it is short. What certainly fails is the pause while we wait for the picture to arrive— "The great engine room . . . with its new turbines . . . and the mechanics waiting for . . . the order to start up." You simply have to bridge that gap with words.

Starting and Stopping

But of course a film does not want solid commentary throughout—on the contrary, few can survive it. There comes a point in an incessant commentary when the mind simply refuses to accept any more information through the ears. Some films need no commentary at all. Most need some commentary and some silence. And then you are right up against the question of starting and stopping. You need some sort of reason for both. If you have written over a picture sequence and then stopped, it is slightly odd to come in over the same sequence with a piece of commentary that could just as well have been given in the earlier paragraph, even if it's just a few more facts. A change of sequence is a perfect reason for starting the talking again, but if it does not change you must make it appear that somehow the visual story has now developed a bit and so there is now something further to say. It means picking up the actual shot with the first half of your first sentence. If there is a sequence change it is a good idea to start a second or two before the shot changes. It avoids the lantern lecture look—waiting for the fresh slide and starting again. Also it flows well if, say, the fourth or fifth word exactly fits the new picture; for example, "From Athens to the harbor is five miles"; if the picture cuts from the city to the harbor on the word "harbor" it makes the viewer less conscious of the visual jerk by covering it with interlocked words. It does something else too. It gives the sound recordist a chance to mix from his traffic disc to his surf and sea gulls disc while the commentator's voice is distracting the ear from his artifice. If you held back your commentary till the shot of the harbor had come up, the sound effects mix would be far more noticeable.

And just as you need some sort of implied excuse for starting, so you need one for stopping. Again, this will come out of your last phrase—something that directs the viewer's attention back at the picture exclusively. It is sometimes called the throw-line—a half sentence that throws the picture up in the air to be looked at. The last half of the last sentence, you may have noticed, is by far the most important in any paragraph of commentary. It is the bit that goes ringing round your head as you watch the pictures that follow and colors your attitude to them. If the sequence is a boat in a rough sea, those last words can make the sequence seem one of danger, or of seasickness, or just bad fishing weather, depending on what they are. The effects and music will help too, and it is an illustration of the fact that writing is not easily divisible from production—writing the correct throw-line at the right point and then leaving it to pictures and effects or music is part of production skill.

The throw-line is an instance of the most important part of commentary writing—the business of improving the pictures. One instance—a travel film—a dull shot of people wading across a stream. But the last sentence of the previous paragraph was that two crocodiles had been seen in that part of the stream the day before, and the dull shot becomes very interesting indeed. There are many ways of making pictures better—by adding facts, adding suspense, adding an attitude, suggesting a parallel image—a simile which makes the whole sequence more enjoyable—and it is here that the art of film commentary lies. When you are doing this, you really are blending picture and word so that both together achieve an effect that neither could achieve separately. And if you can master it, you have in your hands one of the most powerful means of communication in the world.

Appendix

Summary of Procedure

1. Convene first meeting and invite:
   a. Expert on the subject.
   b. Expert on the audience.
2. First planning meeting.
   a. Purpose:
      (1) To formulate precise objectives.
      (2) To formulate desired audience response.
      (3) To select a presentation team.
      (4) To draft a logical sequence.
      (5) To decide audience size and who should be invited.
      (6) To choose a location.
      (7) To fix the date.
   b. Action:
      (1) Book location for dress rehearsal and presentation.
      (2) Invite the audience.
      (3) Fix the date of the next meeting.
      (4) Invite presentation team to next meeting.
      (5) Circulate to all members of next meeting the decisions (1) to (7) made at this one.
3. Second planning meeting.
   a. Purpose:
      (1) To work through the logical sequence.

    (2) To confirm the running order, duration, and breaks.

    (3) To agree to each presenter's objective.

    (4) To agree to each presenter's content.

    (5) To discuss major demonstrations for inclusion.

    (6) To discuss supporting documentation.

    (7) To list future meetings and their purpose, including date of run-through.

  b. Action:

    (1) Initiate preparation of major demonstrations.

    (2) Initiate the writing of supporting documents.

    (3) Initiate logistics—for example:

      (a) Welcoming arrangements.

      (b) Meals and refreshments.

      (c) Transportation.

      (d) Displays.

      (e) Folders.

    (4) Fix the date of the next meeting with all concerned.

    (5) Invite a probable member of the audience.

  c. Action of each presenter:

    (1) Appoint understudy.

    (2) Write out full notes of intended content and submit them to group before the next meeting.

4. Third planning meeting.

  a. Purpose:

    (1) To go through all the presenters' notes.

    (2) To eliminate contradiction, overlap, and gaps.

    (3) To discuss all presentations from point of view of audience and see where this will necessitate omission, expansion, or contraction.

    (4) To cross-fertilize and give all presenters a chance to make suggestions about the whole presentation.

  b. Action: Fix production session with each presenter and the production manager.

  c. Action of each presenter:

    (1) Dictate presentation into tape recorder (maximum duration two-thirds of allotted time) and get it transcribed.

    (2) Write in suggested audio-visual aids.

5. Production sessions with each presenter.
   a. Purpose:
      (1) To establish duration of each presentation.
      (2) To make any necessary cuts.
      (3) To insure that each presentation is well structured.
      (4) To insure proper texturing.
      (5) To check presentations against attention curve.
      (6) To discuss content and initiate production of all audio-visual aids.
   b. Action:
      (1) Order all audio-visual aids and establish their delivery date.
      (2) Give final script instructions to presenters.
      (3) Fix date for stagger-through when all audio-visual aids are ready.
   c. Action of each presenter: Finalize script and check it within the duration time allotted.
6. Stagger-through with each presenter separately.
   a. Purpose:
      (1) To check that all visuals are correctly executed.
      (2) To insure that visuals fit smoothly into the structure and script of the presentation.
      (3) To recheck timing now that visuals are included.
      (4) To enable presenter to identify any problems presented by visuals.
      (5) To judge if each individual presentation will achieve the objective for which it was devised.
   b. Action: Final cuts, alterations, corrections to or omission of visuals.
   c. Action of each presenter: Polish the presentation and privately rehearse complicated visual sequences with understudy.
7. Run-through with everyone present including audience representative.
   a. Purpose:
      (1) To see the entire presentation at the actual speed it will run.
      (2) To establish final timings.

(3) To judge the overall effect of the presentation.

(4) To test all junction-point procedures.

(5) To make final cuts or alterations if required.

(6) To practice all technical and stage management details in conjunction with the presenters—such as lights, slides, demonstrations.

b. Action:

(1) Time each presenter.

(2) Make notes on each presenter.

(3) Go through notes separately with each presenter at the end. (No interruptions.)

8. Dress rehearsal.

a. Purpose:

(1) To test the whole presentation in the actual location, under the actual conditions, and with the actual equipment to be used.

(2) To familiarize the presenters with the circumstances they will encounter.

(3) To give everyone practice and confidence.

b. Action: Times and notes as at run-through.

9. Presentation day.

a. Arrive in good time.

b. Each presenter checks through all his own audio-visual aids.

c. Have informal meeting between presenters and audience.

d. Take technical upsets lightheartedly.

e. Each presenter should meet a week later and discuss the lessons that can be learned.

Checklist

STRUCTURE

Is the presentation too long?
Do the first two minutes set the right tone for the speaker's acceptance by the audience?
Does the argument start from the audience's level of knowledge, interest, and understanding?
Does a clear reason why the audience should be interested emerge early enough?
Does it make them want to know?
Are there enough intermediate summaries and signposts?
Is there too much straight factual assertion?
Is it too comprehensive?
Are there too many details which should be in supporting documents?
Is the last sentence the right one to leave in the audience's heads?

TEXTURE

Are there intriguing peeps behind the curtain?
Could the audience be brought into the presentation in some way?
Are the visuals spaced for best sustaining interest?
Are there long dull patches?
Can the middle trough be raised by any questions or participation?
Does it contain too much visual dodging about?

IMPACT

Are the most important points sufficiently memorable?
Can they be given special impact?
Are there pictures of everything that you want remembered?

USE OF WORDS

Does it sound as if a written document is being read?
Are there any "literary" phrases that no one ever uses in conversation?
Is it studiously avoiding "I" and "you"?
Is it overgrammatical?
Is the word order right for easy understanding?
Are there enough questions stated before answers are given?
Are the sentences too long? (Look suspiciously at anything more than two or three lines long.)
Are there too many abstract nouns?
Are there enough examples and analogies?
Does it assume the audience knows more than it does?
Is it insultingly oversimplified?
Should more background facts be casually dropped in?
Does it repeat itself?
Is it padded out with unnecessary verbiage?
Is it clear and unambiguous?
Is it too cryptic and compressed?

DELIVERY

Is the presenter speaking loud enough?
Does he drop his voice at the end of sentences?
Is his chin too close to his chest?
Does he tend to gabble, mumble, or talk at the blackboard?
Any distracting physical or verbal mannerisms? (But don't worry unless they really do distract.)

AUDIO-VISUAL AIDS

Is the visual aid necessary?
Is it genuinely visual or just a visible verbal?
Blackboard
  Chalk color?
  Presenter's positioning?

Use of pointer?
Long spells of drawing?
Board properly cleared?
Properly stable?

Pad
Sheet disposal; wastebox nearby?

Charts
Drawings clear enough?
Large enough?
Simple enough?
Interleaves included?

Magnetic boards and the like
Build up too slow?
Too many pieces to search through?

Solid objects
Are there enough?
Could there be more displayed or distributed?

Working models and demonstrations
Will they be there in time to be checked properly?
Will there be time to take action if they fail?
Is there time for sufficient rehearsal with them?
Fire regulations, power supply, ventilation?

Overhead projectors
Keystoning effect (tilt screen if necessary)?
Noise of fan?
Obstruction of vision?

Slides—content
Too verbal?
Too much information included?
Too complicated visually?
Too crowded?
Sufficient use of color?
Left on screen too long?
Properly explained by presenter?

Slides—operations
Spare projector?
Duplicate slides?
Proper rehearsal time for actual projector?

Do slides fit?
Will arc burn them?
Rehearsal for projectionist?
Agreed signals to projectionist?
Agreed breakdown procedures?
Reloads of slides avoided?

Film
Is it really appropriate?
Does it run too long?
Is it properly placed for maximum interest and effect?

Audience

Right number?
Too many?
Too few?
Are presenters experienced with this size audience?
Should the presentation be given more times to fewer people?
Do you want the audience compact or scattered?
Lights on or off?
Proper deference by speaker?
Wrestling or judo?
Questions or no questions?
If there are to be questions, when?

One-man Presentation

Encourage questions throughout.
Proceed by dialog.
Plan the order of points to be made.
Informal rehearsal.
Prepare introduction.
Extreme simplification of visuals.

Venue

Own building if possible.

Avoid too vast a room.

Wide or narrow frontage for seats?

Not too wide a gap between speaker and front row.

Check technical facilities.

Signpost rooms and corridors.

Distractions from doors and windows; is presentation at the right end of the room?

For strange venue, check with someone who has used it before.

STAGE

Lights

Are all charts and speakers clearly lit?

Does light spill onto screen?

Is light in speaker's eyes?

Are lamps too high?

Decor

Colored draperies or flats (screens)?

Uniformity of furniture?

Display panels?

Layout

Sight lines; check for masking.

Does the stage look appetizing?

Stage management

What happens at junction points?

Microphone procedure.

Film order and cues.

Slide order and cues.

Charts, or whatever, to be set or struck during presentation?

Doors closed and warning notices on outside.

Go right through full script for every requirement.

Ask the "what if . . . ?" questions.

Chalk, string, cellophane tape, wire, and the like.

Check for internal (fire drill and such) and external interruptions (school playground outside window, for example).